THE PENDANT

Bella J Murray

First in the Stones Trilogy.

Published By Davidson Print UK

ISBN: 978-0-9933831-0-6

To all my Family and Friends who has been with me on this journey.
I couldn't have done it without you.

SYNOPSIS

Melissa, beautiful and intelligent, having just lost her mother

comes into a large

inheritance.

Adam, smooth and charming, hides his true nature from

those he knows and is driven by

the need to possess.

Suzy, spontaneous and witty, has a secret that not even she

knows about

about.

Conrad, handsome and smart, is set on a path of discovery

and is forced to question his

beliefs.

PROLOGUE

They stood face to face...not moving...not breathing...just waiting...until the tinkling strains of a babes cry could be heard. Just as the first sounds pierced the realm and allowed her a moment of victory there was a second cry and her eyes widened in fear. He shifted into his natural form but not before he caught her expression. It was just enough to give him pause and as she stood there motionless his thick black fog surrounded her enveloping her and hid her from the others whom watched nervously from the protection of their stones. As he brushed past her ear his words reverberated in her mind ..."Ah...it has now begun...'

CHAPTER ONE

Blood dripped slowly and silently from the elegantly long finger that was only just visible beneath the long silver cloak that covered it. Her steps were like whispers on the frozen ground and as she breathed icy puffs of air left her blood red human lips. She briefly contemplated the reasons for choosing a human form this night but was increasingly aware of the questioning eyes boring into her as they watched and waited. Sensing a mixture of awe and mistrust at her human form from those around her, she could only wonder if she had done the right thing. The chanting began again quietly then rose loudly then stopped. They were waiting and watching her every move. It had been over a millennia since the dark and light magic had been this strong. T'would be two strong souls born this eve...she thought privately. Those surrounding her gathered once every hundred years to aid and witness the birth of twinned souls. It was a most rare and beautiful thing. She shivered slightly, not from the cold but from the magic surrounding her. The chanting had started again but softly, haunting and beautiful in the cold night air. The moon glistened and reflected off the huge tablets of stone that stood erect in this secret, mystical place. Each one bore the mark of the elder it represented and appeared when their time had come to an end. It was both sanctuary and a tomb for a hundred years at a time. Only those twinned souls that find each other in each and every lifetime gives continued life to the chosen one and also the ability to create souls.

She was well aware of their presence as the vibrations surrounding her contained their pure essence and magical power. She glanced around at those whose eyes she could feel and noted that while some looked almost bored others looked nervous. The way they positioned themselves on or near their mark told her all she needed to know. Their ethereal forms could easily be mistaken for angels. Beautiful beyond words it was impossible for any other being to look upon their form without being bathed in a dazzling rainbow of glittering dust. She almost smiled when she caught some that were slouched against their mark and again at the others who were tapping a foot or drumming their fingers while sat on the top or against their marks. In a way she could not blame them. She had outlived them all. They had once stood where she stood now and when it was over they became enslaved to their mark. Destined to give up their essence and bear witness to this ritual for more years than she cared to count.

Her human footfalls barely make a print on the icy snow beneath her as she glides over the sacred ground. She can feel the powerful vibration of magic pulsating through her body as she reaches the giant stone in front of her. Standing proud and majestic at nearly 12 feet tall the giant stone, pale grey in the moonlight, hummed with magic. She dipped her fingers once more into the glowing green goblet made of exquisite Moldavite. A mystical, clear glass the colour of deep forest green and almost luminous when held up to the moon. The heat and vibrations of the Moldavite in her hand gave her an intense feeling of fulfilment and love and her body began to hum with the thousand voices of the elders who communicated with her through this precious gemstone. The blood was warm to the touch and contained not just her own essence but the essence of all those that had gone before her. Her mind was heavy with cascading thoughts; some made sense and were glimpses of the future but some made no sense at all but made her responsibilities now feel like Thor's Hammer pressing down upon her skull. With warring thoughts and an overflowing heart she sighed as this was what she had been chosen for.

Gently she placed her bloodied finger upon the dark symbols on the last of the magnificent stones and felt them writher and move across the smooth glacier like facade.

Overhead the moon shone a direct path through the misty grey snow clouds to where she stood. A burst of lightening hot heat that would have incinerated a normal human penetrated her finger tip and illuminated her from the inside out while it pushed its way to her very core opening and flooding her soul with the oldest and most powerful magic known only to those within the higher realm. To a mere mortal they could be forgiven for thinking they were witnessing the birth of an angel as high up in the air in the centre of the moons beam, head flung back, back arched and arms open wide, the force of magic continued to pulsate through her body illuminating her from the inside. She was being exquisitely filled with love so powerful, intense and blinding that all beings within the realm felt a sudden shift in the air and an unexplained warmth on their skin. For not even those who lived and travelled between realms knew the secret of how or when twinned souls were created. She was a myth even to those who were gifted with their own mystical powers such as the Fey. They only knew what the rest of the inhabitants of all the other realms knew;

that it was a rare and precious thing envied by some and embraced by others. Some humans believed it so fiercely that they wrote books trying to explain the meaning of true mates and oft would spend a lifetime searching for their twinned soul. It was this very reason that the Fey had remained interested in the human race instead of destroying it.

What they did not know was that it was her and her alone who had the power to create souls within this secret, ancient and mystical realm. A vessel for the powerful magic and the one true essence who had the ability to see back to the time of earth's creation and forward to when the earth as we know it would cease to be. It was but one moment in every one hundred years that she most treasured and that was the ritual of a twinned birth; the power of eternal love rushing, pulsating and possessing her and the essence of the elders and herself coming together with passion, knowledge and magic to create the very thing that gives humans the hope of love eternal.

With a brilliant flash of light her human form once again touched the icy ground and without leaving a footprint she made her way to the centre of the circle. The observers were now silent and in awe of what they were about to witness despite having witnessed it for a millennia. The air became still and the vibrations of magic became a distant hum in the background enveloping her like a soft caress. Raising her arms towards the moon she started to whisper words from an ancient tongue repeating them over and over. Out of the corner of her eye she glimpsed the first rays of sunlight and swiftly turned her attention back to the moon. The observers began to chant loudly rising and falling with each human breath she took.

The chanting stopped abruptly and while she stood in the centre of the mystic circle with both the sun's first rays and the moon's last beams she reached inside her silver and almost pearlescent cloak that shimmered in the new light and from within the folds she gently grasped the two pulsating orbs that shone brightly in a musical dance of multi-coloured shades too beautiful to describe. While they spun and spiralled in front of her she penetrated each one with her mind, probing and checking that the first bond had formed between them. A gentle sigh escaped her lips and with a smile she caught glimpses of their journey through their first life. She felt a jolt when one of the souls probed back. Delighted but stunned she shook her head and almost tutted in a human fashion. ...Theirs would be a strong bond indeed. She and their watchers would have to keep a careful eye on these two...

Pathways were already forming between the souls as they danced and circled above her head. Some were already beginning to forge the love these two would share while others included wisdom, fulfilment, passion, strength and mischievousness...She quickly hid a small secret smile just as it appeared as with a gentle sweep of her hand she summoned a tiny piece of each soul. Peering at their tiny sparkling forms she began to weave the words needed to form her twinned souls' watchers and protectors. Instead of being infused with love and passion for another soul they were infused with courage, strength, wisdom and knowledge that would enable them to guide the twinned souls in each lifetime. Joining her in unison her observers began chanting while leaning in only to stop abruptly as the ancient words spilled from her lips once more . The tiny pieces of the twinned souls that she had summoned became souls in their own right in a blinding flash of colourful light magic. As she raised the watcher souls and sent them towards the heavens she continued to murmur ancient words of love and protection that would bind them to not just her but to the souls they had been born to watch. She then turned her attention back to the twinned souls to send them on the journey.

One of these would be trouble...she thought as she plucked the first soul from its spiralling dance in the air above her to cup it within both of her hands. She held it gently and breathed life into the soul so that it could be born into the human world...You are going to be a mischievous one...

As she watched it shoot into the sky above, leaving a trail of magical dust behind it, she quickly reached out to grab the second soul before it tried to follow its mate in a flurry of light and spitting magical sparks. As she cupped the second soul she whispered calming words and summoning her power she drew a deep breath while in her mind's eye she followed the trail of love and magic through the realms until she heard the single tinkling cry of a babe.

Just as she was about to breath life into this second soul she felt small vibrations of dark magic in the ground beneath her human feet. Gripping the soul in her hands more tightly she sensed the observers impatience and fear and tried to block the effects of the dark magic that was threatening to penetrate this secret place and the precious soul she held now closely to her lips. The dark magic was strong as she knew it would be for it mirrored the light magic of the souls she had created this night. She felt the ground beneath her grow colder and heard the observers chanting getting louder. The breath she held escaped before she could fill the precious soul with its life-force. The soul in her hands sensed her fear and tried to fight its way to its mate but she held fast as without its first breath received from her body the soul would not live and go to its destined human host to find its mate.

She felt the sudden shift as she finally thought she had blocked the dark magic from entering her secret domain and was only semi-consciously aware that the observers chanting had stopped waiting for her to repeat the ancient words while she drew in a second breath. Time stopped... which she never thought possible unless it was her own doing and as the breath left her lips to fill the soul in front of her the dark magic ravaged through her domain as she let go of the second soul abruptly. Watching the trail of magical dust that could not be dimmed by the dark magic that now covered the circle where she stood she could not be certain if she had succeeded in sending the soul to the destined human for there in front of her was the master of dark magic himself.

The observer's spirits disappeared back into their stones and she was left exposed and vulnerable. Oh they had come face to face many times over the centuries and always when twin souls were born. Never yet had he succeeded in destroying her but the shift she had felt and the speed he had penetrated the sacred realm made her fear for the first time that his power would prevent her souls from finding each other. She didn't move and could not breath as he circled her slowly taking on a human form himself while appraising her from head to toe. For as powerful as she was, he was her equal.

"Well... Well... The human form suits you... " His mouth did not move but his words reverberated in the air around them. Still she held her breath as he came to stop and stand directly in front of her. Lifting her chin almost lovingly so that she could see the last of the now faint magical trail of the second soul. She blocked him from her mind as she prayed the second soul would find its host and pushed his hand away from her chin while looking directly into his eyes and his soul. There was nothing to see as she knew there wouldn't be, just an empty black, shimmering, swirling mass that undulated and beckoned you into its depths.

They stood face to face...not moving...not breathing...just waiting...until the tinkling strains of a babe's cry could be heard. Just as the first sounds pierced the realm and allowed her a moment of victory there was a second cry and her eyes widened in fear. He shifted into his natural form but not before he caught her expression. It was just enough to give him pause and as she stood there motionless his thick black fog surrounded her enveloping her and hid her from the others who watched nervously from the protection of their stones. As he brushed past her ear his words reverberated in her mind ..."Ah...it has now begun...'

CHAPTER TWO

She held close to her heart the tear-stained and slightly crumpled note his good friend had secretly given her. The moon cast a silvery path to the entrance of the now empty croft where she had once lived. Pulling the plaid up over her head and wrapping it tighter around her body she made her way undetected to the place he wanted to meet. Her breath came in short gasps as her heartbeat drummed inside her chest echoing each footstep she took. Her body trembled not from the cold but from remembering the words he had written:

...I go tae dae battle at first light, tis now I ask of ye a boon. Tis my heart desires for ye to ken, that I hae loved ye, ever since I was a wee lad, I ken not wha will happen, but many a' blood will be split on these bonnie braes. I dae ken that should it be my blood split, god will grant me nae peace unless I git tae hold ye in my arms while whispering the words my heart begs ye tae hear. Tis a dangerous thing that I ken, tae ask ye to come to your auld home. Should anyone see us, ye ken what will happen. Ne'er would I want ye to come tae harm, so tis for ye to decide. I will be waiting for ye ...

As she reached the door, she slipped the plaid from her head taking one last look around before she opened the door, not noticing the slight movement from where she had just come. Once inside she let her plaid slip to the ground where she stood astonished at the sight before her. Coming to stand behind her he watched as she glanced around in wonder. The room had been transformed from an empty, cold, disused space to an intimate place made for lovers. He had lit a small fire in the hearth, the smell of pine and peat scenting the air. Light from the embers cast a warm glow along the freshly laid rushes on the stone floor. He had hung tapestries over the windows to keep in the warmth. The slight breeze from outside moved them rhythmically allowing the moonlight to witness their lovers union. He asked her softly to go and sit on the makeshift bed. As she sat down he noticed that she parted her lips slightly in anticipation. Her eyes looked at him in awe. They were iridescent shades of green the likes of which he had never seen before. So taut with emotion and lust he did not hesitate when she beckoned him over.

He took the green gemstone he had scoured the Highlands for from the pouch concealed behind his back. He turned her around slowly and with trembling fingers placed the gem over her head letting it rest between her breasts. Possessively, he fastened the leather bond around her neck. Turning her back to face him his lips joined hers in a moment of pent up, pulsating need, emotion so intense he nearly lost control. She felt his raw primitive lust, along with the love he had denied for so long, strip away all the barriers she had erected and fill her with such exquisite passion that she surrendered her heart with a will that matched his...

Melissa woke with a start and sat up wiping the beads of sweat from her brow. Dazed from waking so abruptly she caressed the pendant she had worn since her mother's death finding comfort in the smoothness. Feeling a little calmer, she wondered what could have caused her to wake suddenly...had she been dreaming? Looking at her bedside clock, she saw it was nearly seven am. Reluctantly she climbed out of bed and walked into the bathroom to take a shower. A few minutes later, feeling refreshed and awake, she put on her clothes, dried her hair and grabbed her toothbrush from the bathroom putting it in the holdall she had packed the previous night. Glancing around her bedroom one more time she did a mental checklist of everything she would need. Satisfied that she had not forgotten anything she picked up the holdall and went downstairs. Not feeling like her customary strong coffee this morning she just picked her keys up from the side table and left her modest mews cottage in a small suburb of Oxford to go to what was her parents home less than twenty miles away.

As she pulled up outside the huge mansion she sat for a few moments in her car taking steadying deep breaths. It was the first time she had come here since the terrible news. 'It's now or never' she thought as she stepped from the car and slowly approached the main door. Letting herself in Melissa dropped her holdall on the floor where she stood. The loss of her mother, combined with being back at her childhood home, hit her with more force than she had ever imagined. Tears began to stream down her face as she looked around her. Furniture and paintings that had graced the rooms were now hidden from view covered by white sheets. There was no warmth or friendly shouts to welcome her and the faint scent of her mother hung in the air as a lasting reminder. Removing all the sheets as she mindlessly walked past she made her way up the grand staircase and along the landing towards her parents room. The tears abated as she stood at the door. She could almost hear her mother's voice coming from behind her.

"Melissa, it is extremely rude to stand outside someone's bedroom door! What goes on behind closed doors are of no concern to a child. Now run along and see to that puppy of yours before it can get up to any more mischief!"

"Yes mother, I'll go and see to him." Melissa chuckled softly to herself remembering her mother's stern reprimands and her meek replies. Although she was sometimes harsh the love and friendship between them grew stronger as she grew older. They did almost everything together. She gently placed her hand on the door and was sad for a moment knowing that she would never hear her mother's voice again. Melissa lowered her hand to the ornate crystal orb caressing it slightly as she turned it and then pushed the door open.

The sweet scent of lavender and rose water still lingered faintly in the air as Melissa took a deep breath and let out a heavy sigh gingerly wiping a lone tear that was beginning to make a silent descent down her cheek. She stood where she was for a moment afraid to let a torrent of tears follow. Slowly walking into the room she made her way to the huge canopied bed and lovingly stroked the pillow. "Oh mother...why now?" Melissa heard her own anguished whisper escape but knew her mother would not answer. She stepped away from the bed and walked over to the dressing table. Briefly, she imagined that if she sat down and looked in the mirror her mother would be standing there right behind her. She lifted a stray lock away from her eyes and stared at her reflection. People often remarked on her beauty although while studying for her degree in history it was more of a hindrance. She was tall and slender with long dark curls that framed the often mistaken aristocratic features of her face; A slender nose slightly upturned at the end, a mouth that Melissa often complained was too big but that was in fact sensuous and delicately formed high cheekbones, which enhanced her heart shaped face. The resemblance to her mother was nearly painful to see as she sat staring at the mirror. The only difference was their eyes. When peering closer to her reflection Melissa blinked, opened them wider, and briefly wondered why she did not inherit her parents blue eyes. Her fingers trailed a line across the top of the glass and her gaze drifted to a half-full bottle of her mother's perfume. Refusing to evoke any more memories she turned away. Melissa turned her attention to the drawers, hesitated for just a moment, and pulled the first draw open.

Curiosity, her mother had told her, was an unseemly trait. Melissa just could not help herself she had always been curious. Her parents would either find her exploring one of the many 'nooks and crannies' of the huge Georgian mansion or beside the large tranquil lake with a gently cascading waterfall, which was surrounded by landscaped gardens and forestry. Some people even remarked that 'it was twice the size of Buckingham palace'. It had four floors with two end wings giving it an almost 'u' shape. Each room had priceless paintings and antique furniture mixed with a contemporary décor. Her mother's creative style had soon become a business venture as her wealthy friends, some of which included famous movie stars and even members of royalty, often commissioned her mother to re-style their own homes. It also had endless passageways and countless rooms to get lost in not unlike a private playground. Her mother's bedroom was one of the few rooms where Melissa had been forbidden to enter as a child unless directed to do so even as a teenager. Not until she was sixteen did her mother allow her in when she would be dressing for the opera or one of the many grand parties that took place in the ballroom. Sixteen was the age her mother deemed her old enough to be a part of that social world and allowed to mix with the nobility and wealthy businessmen who often attended one of the Conway's exclusive parties. Even though her mother came across as aloof Melissa never felt that her behaviour in this respect was odd. It was just the way it was despite it being 1993.

Now twelve years later Melissa was twenty-eight. Although she had attended many of the parties that graced the rooms of her home, and met many eligible bachelors, she always let her mother down gently. Every time her mother tried to matchmake Melissa used the same excuses -- she wanted to live a little, experience different things, maybe even get to see some of the world before she married. The only thing she omitted every time was that none of the men her mother introduced to her seemed right. Melissa could never quite explain the feeling she got, not even to herself. Her mother's aloofness would cause her to just raise one eyebrow and wander off in a different direction. Slowly Melissa's mouth began to curl upwards at her memories. Her father, a quiet, intelligent man, was a renowned historian who had many books published and was often asked to lecture in universities all over the world. He used to berate her mother gently telling her that it was only natural that a child with such an inquisitive nature should have its curiosity roused at its surroundings and want to grow up and explore further afield believing that you were never too old to get married.

Taking out papers that were all neatly folded in the draw she spread them out in front of her. Her father's death certificate was among the papers and she thought about how heart broken he would have been about her mother's death if he had have outlived her. For an instant she was almost glad that her father had passed away five years before. For a time Melissa just sat there holding her parents death certificates refusing to let the loneliness engulf her. Instead she thought, in a bittersweet way, they had found each other again and wondered if it was indeed at all possible, or was she just being fanciful? Contemplating the differences between her parents she thought they actually complimented each other even though her father was twenty years her mother's senior and they were nearly opposites in every way. Putting the death certificates to one side she started flipping through the remaining sheets; nothing but statements and old bills so she placed them gently back into the draw laying the certificates gently on top. Melissa pulled open one draw after another and found more letters, disused make-up and trinkets.

She sighed heavily remembering the polite and sympathetic words of the two police officers that had knocked on the door to her flat in Oxford three weeks ago.

"Miss Conway, I am PC Matthews and this is WPC Hawley. Can we come in?" WPC Hawley, quite petite for a police officer, looked thoughtful as she led Melissa back inside to the large but cosy kitchen.

"Would you like to sit down Miss Conway?" She asked hesitantly. Melissa took a couple of steps backwards and sat on one of the high stools. She clasped her hands together in her lap to stop herself from fidgeting knowing it could only be bad news. After all, she thought, the police do not knock on your door and invite you to take a seat if they are going to tell you something good, do they? PC Mathews took a step forward and taking his cue from WPC Hawley he came straight to the point.

"I'm very sorry Miss Conway but I regret to inform you that your mother has been in a tragic accident." Clearing his throat he said quite quickly. "She was pronounced dead at the scene." Melissa visibly paled. She gripped the counter next to her knowing there was worse to come. WPC Hawley started to go to Melissa's aid but with one hand still resting on the counter Melissa raised her other hand to stop her. WPC Hawley glanced behind her at PC Mathews, who nodded, and so she retreated slowly back to where she was previously standing. PC Mathews, feeling highly inadequate at this sort of thing, hoped he would not make a hash of it and continued where he left off.

"We recognised the car by the number plate..." Feeling even more uncomfortable by the second he tugged loosely at his collar "umm...well what little was left of it." Abruptly he placed his hands behind him thinking he had managed at least the first part quite well. WPC Hawley raised her eyebrows in disbelief especially since she had warned him to be sensitive about situations like these. Catching the look she cast him he blurted out "sorry again Miss Conway!" Melissa, oblivious to the blush staining his cheeks and the way he seemed to be squirming on the spot as he realised he had indeed made a hash of it, could only see the wreckage of her mother's car. Almost as if she was standing at the scene she began to shiver uncontrollably. This time she did not object when WPC Hawley went to comfort her. Taking one of Melissa's hands in her own she spoke quietly and authoritatively. PC Mathews stumbled backwards into a chair and promptly sat wishing the ground would open up and swallow him. PC Hawley, ignoring him, turned her attention back to Melissa.

"Have you any family or perhaps a close friend you would like me to contact, as you really shouldn't be alone at a time like this?"

"No!" Melissa said abruptly, fighting to keep her breathing and voice under control. Desolately, and in a mere whisper, she spoke slowly. .

"No..." she lowered her head trying to win the battle going on inside of her... "It's ok... I...I... just want to be alone for a while..." She did not want to know but desperately needing this to be over with she paused for a few minutes before she found the courage to ask how it happened. "Tell me..." "How...how... did... did... it happen?" PC Mathews looked carefully at Melissa. The resolve she showed earlier had slipped away just as the moon takes over from the sun he thought. No longer was she bathed in the sunlight that made the coppery streaks in her hair glisten and the olive green of her eyes sparkle like the iridescent hues of a rare emerald. Her sunshine had suddenly been extinguished; in its place was the cover of darkness. Her head still slightly bent -- her hands now resting gently on the counter -- shoulders that drooped unable to bear the load that the news had brought her. Melissa looked up from the floor and slowly raised her eyes to face PC Mathews. He had to admire her for the way she stiffened her back summoning all her strength to help her hear the rest of what was being said. He unconsciously looked deep in to her eyes and noticed that they had changed yet again. Her eyes were now the deepest green he had ever seen. Tiny gold flecks now flickered as though in defiance and defeat. The intensity of her stare unnerved him a little more and he looked to WPC Hawley to continue.

"As far as we can make out it looks as though your mother swerved to avoid a deer that darted out from the forest on your parent's estate. Tragically the car hit a tree and exploded, leaving very little I'm afraid...I'm truly sorry Miss Conway." She stepped closer and placed a small leather pouch on the counter. "This was all that remained." She turned and nodded to PC Matthews who was still visibly trying to cover up his embarrassment and his fascination with Melissa's eyes.

"There are bereavement councillors available if you would like me to arrange someone to visit. Just call me on this number." WPC Hawley lay a card down next to the pouch and moments later they left.

A lone tear made its way silently down her face. Pulling herself together while drying her eye she reminded herself it had been three weeks since that awful news. The funeral had been two weeks ago and yet the pain was still raw. Melissa reached down to where she had dropped her bag, rummaged around, and took out a small photograph of her mother. An upbeat rendition of Beethoven suddenly filled the room. Melissa reached down again this time to rummage for her mobile.

"Hi Suzy..." Melissa answered the phone reluctantly, not really wanting to speak to anyone. Suzy heard the sadness in Melissa's voice and determined to bring a smile to her face almost gushed when she spoke.

"Hi honey, where are you? I have some fabulous news to tell you and some good old gossip!" Melissa knew what gossip meant, especially if it came from Suzy, and almost smiled. Then, a little guiltily, answered her.

"I'm at my mother's house." Without waiting for Melissa to draw breath, Suzy pounced. "I'll be there in a hour," and abruptly hung up. She quietly left her mother's bedroom and wandered down the hallway stopping outside her childhood room.

Hesitantly she opened the door. Inside the room was just the same as it had been when she moved out eight years ago. During the last few years she had only stayed in it periodically so had felt no need to redecorate; nor had her parents. Going over to the huge bay window she looked out over the grounds below. As a young girl she had the most vivid daydreams any young girl could have. She chuckled softly to herself remembering the countless times she was a princess locked in a tower by an evil fairy queen waiting for her prince to come. Sitting astride a brilliant white charger he would race towards her tower cutting down all that stood between them be it a dragon or the fairy queen herself. Her father used to love hearing her tales and teased her mercilessly while her mother would tell her to stop being fanciful. Melissa never missed the wondrous and sometimes sad look that passed between them every time she told one of her stories. Peering out again she could almost see the same white charger that used to occupy most of her youthful days. As if her parents were in the room with her she spoke aloud ...I know...I know...and ran her fingertips gently along the window sill before she turned around to make her way back into the hallway. Just as she approached the top of the grand staircase she paused briefly realising she had left her bag. Running back to her mother's room she scooped up her bag and glanced sadly around the room. Letting out a breath she felt a strange tingly sensation as she touched her pendant while shutting the door softly. Then shaking her head she headed back to the staircase and went down in to the great hall.

She wandered aimlessly through the great hall, no longer awed by the priceless paintings which adorned the walls, and in to the kitchen flipping the switch on the kettle as she walked past it. Plopping down at the antique oak table that took precedence in the middle of the vast kitchen area she took the pouch that contained the pendant she now wore and the picture of her mother out of her bag and placed them gently down in front of her. The kettle began to boil but instead of whistling it sounded more like a cat being strangled! She could never understand why her mother had not replaced it and now she never would. Just as a tear threatened to spill, she heard the doorknocker that made the house shake. It must be Suzy she thought. Glad of the reprieve she very nearly chuckled thinking 'God, that woman could smell a coffee a mile off!'

Smiling for the first time in weeks she went to the door and opened it. Suzy hugged Melissa fiercely.

"Just in time I would say" Suzy said as she reluctantly released Melissa and heard the unearthly sound coming from behind them. Without pausing for air she practically dragged Melissa back in to the kitchen unplugging the kettle as she went putting an end to the awful sound. Then spinning around again she surveyed Melissa from head to toe.

"First thing tomorrow morning we are going to pay a visit to the hairdressers.... Hmmm... better stop off at Wiggins too. Oh! Melissa! Just what have you been living on?" She gasped as she opened the fridge door and looked at the meagre contents. Melissa opened her mouth to speak but Suzy shut the fridge door with a flourish. "Hmmm...looks as though we'd better get some groceries in first! Now you make the coffee and I'll be right back" and with that she flounced out of the kitchen. Melissa watched her go still unable to utter a word.

Suzy had been Melissa's friend since they were twelve. They had shared all their secrets, dreams, and fears in the small room they occupied for four years at St Josephs, a private school for girls set in the heart of

London. Both were snubbed by their fellow pupils most of whom came from titled families. Feeling lost amongst their peers they bonded instantly knowing what one was going to say to the other before they said it. They both blossomed into the most striking pair of females ever to grace the streets of both Oxford and London. Although the same height Melissa's long curly dark hair and eyes a rare shade of green contrasted vividly with Suzy's sleek blond bob and sunshine blue eyes.

Often the attention they received was unwelcome and was probably another reason she had stayed single. Suzy on the other hand, who Melissa thought made the saying 'variety was the spice of life' an understatement, thought she had found her Mr right again! Melissa only hoped that this one lasted longer than a month! Just as she was about to sink lower in to the chair and reminisce some more she heard the front door bang open announcing Suzy's return. Melissa reluctantly got up and went to help Suzy with the groceries.

"Blimey Suzy, you've bought the whole supermarket!"

"A girl's got to eat honey! You take these bags through. I'm just going to get the rest"

"Rest..?" There's enough here to feed us for a month!" Melissa stood, surrounded by bags, and watched as Suzy demurely disappeared in to the boot of her car nearly falling back out again pulling a huge suitcase, which almost landed on top of her.

"Thought I'd stay with you a while. I think you've had enough time on your own, plus I could do with some moral support too..." the last bit said in typically 'Suzy is single again' mode.

"Oh Suzy, I'm sorry."

"What an earth for? Richard was a blip in my busy schedule and a few other things besides." She held her hands up in mock surrender laughing as she took in the look on Melissa's face. "Anyway I have a much more urgent matter to attend too."

"Oh, and what might that be?" Melissa stated matter-of-factly, a slight smile hovering on her lips.

"Oh she says! You... You great ninny! Here you are in this huge old house all by yourself, no family..." Suzy broke off abruptly. "Shit...I'm sorry...bloody hell...oh double shit. I cannot help myself...forgive me I can be so bloody tactless at times it is frightening! I just thought I would try and cheer you up a little...you know, help try and take your mind off things for a bit, but no...I go and remind you that you are..." Suzy just about caught herself again and looked skywards waiting for a bolt of lightning to strike her. Seeing her best friend looking so sheepish Melissa took a deep breath and walked over to Suzy giving her arm a reassuring squeeze.

"It's OK... you've cheered me up just by being here and by being tactless!" Suzy looked up into two pools of green,whose depth seemed never ending and smiled shakily. She often wondered what she had done to deserve a friend like Melissa. After unpacking the shopping Suzy cooked her speciality: well, the only thing she could cook without burning: Macaroni cheese. It brought back happier memories of when they roomed together. Melissa, feeling relaxed and a little happier, finally found her appetite and managed to finish the meal in one sitting.

"Have you thought about what you are going to do now, Mel?" Suzy asked.

"I received a letter from my parents' solicitor, Conrad Mackenzie. He has asked if it's possible for him to come and read the will in two days time. I guess it will be a standard affair. There are no other siblings, no other..." Melissa could not quite get the word family out and swallowed audibly before she continued. "There's... only a few charities that my mother supported but it will mean it's... the end." Suzy cursed herself for her earlier remark and did not dare offer a reply just yet. She did not miss the sad look that crossed Melissa's face or the tears that began to surface. Looking away from Suzy she spoke so quietly, it was barely a whisper.

"I don't know what I'm going to do Suzy".

CHAPTER THREE

Conrad Mackenzie felt the small hairs at the nape of his neck stand erect as he stood outside Fairwinds Manor wishing he could be anywhere else. He came from a long line of Mackenzie's and could trace his family back generations. Conrad had decided when he was a young boy to follow in the steps of his father. He was fascinated with all aspects of the Law and felt that justice... sometimes needed a helping hand. As he became older his intuition played a major part in his success. Not only did his sheer size intimidate others but most also remarked on his 'sixth-sense' as some would call it. Conrad, being rather modest, put it down to being lucky and being a factual man thought most people talked a lot of nonsense. His success in the courtroom gained him more than wealth. It gave him a reputation that was almost becoming legendary. 'Mackenzie & Sons' was a very highly respected law firm. The main office had stood for nearly four centuries in the heart of London, since the reign of James I, covertly protecting the archives and artefacts buried deep in the vaults underneath. It also had offices in Oxford and Edinburgh.

Conrad hated this part of the job. The grief was either still horribly raw or families argued selfishly over what they deemed to be theirs. He took a deep breath mentally checking off all the contents of his case making sure he had not forgotten anything, cursing silently at himself. He never forgot anything! Conrad, almost grinning, walked decisively up to the huge double door raising the eagle headed knocker and bringing the beak down with a resounding thud as it found its target. While he waited for the door to be answered he relaxed slightly letting his intuition probe the surroundings. He felt as though something was out of place... strange... he thought, and unable to make sense of it let the feeling go. At least he would not have to stay long. Families tended to hurry these things up so they could begin arguing amongst themselves. He felt a sudden shiver and though his mind wanted to analyse the feeling further he just shrugged it off wanting to get this finished as quickly and neatly as possible. It was only a reading of the will, nothing more for god's sake, he thought.

"Are you sure you're going to be ok?" Suzy asked, nearly jumping out of her skin at the sound of the door.

"Yes...I think so". Linking hands Melissa looked at Suzy, "yes, I'll be ok."

Walking through the hall together, Suzy looked at Melissa once more before releasing her to open the door.

"Hello, I'm Conrad Mackenzie. You must be Melissa. I'm sorry we have to meet under these circumstances." Automatically he held out his hand.

"Well, hello, Conrad! Unfortunately, I'm not Melissa. I'm Suzy...wow...you're not what we...I mean I expected...oh! ...I'm most pleased to meet you." God, he was gorgeous with a capital G! She thought, momentarily forgetting who Conrad was and that Melissa was standing right beside her. It was a few moments before she opened the door wider and made a sweeping gesture towards Melissa. At the sight of the man in front of her, Melissa's body suddenly tensed and instinctively she straightened her spine, a slight scowl on her face.

"Please accept my deepest apologies" Conrad said, thinking that she had frowned due to his error. Immediately he took Melissa's hand in his own. She was breathtaking... even with a scowl upon her face, he silently mused. Maybe... this would not be over as quickly as he first thought.

The instant he clasped her hand his body reeled in shock and amazement. A wild storm of emotions exploded throughout his body almost splitting his skull in two shaking him to the core. He abruptly let go. The hairs on the back of his neck stood to attention while a torrent of shivers ran down his spine. A searing heat penetrated his skin where their hands had touched and almost burned him from within. Melissa pulled her hand back just as quickly feeling what she could only describe as a sudden electric spark. Frightened and bewildered, and feeling a little unsteady, she turned away quickly. Conrad, not all together feeling as composed as he should be, instantly seemed to regret her turning away. He followed them through the great hall while trying to rationalise what had just taken place. Maybe it was just, 'one of those freak of nature things', he had read about recently. Suzy disappeared and returned an instant later carrying three glasses and a bottle of vodka. As they turned to see what she had brought with her, Suzy shrugged her shoulders murmuring, "well, you know...just in case!" Looking all wide eyed and innocent she put the tray down on the side table. Conrad took that as his cue and went around behind the antique desk that dominated the study.

As he sat down his fingers automatically reached out to caress the intricate carvings that had been engraved to frame the surface of the desk.

"No one knows how old it is." Melissa said with a slight arch of her eyebrow.

"How did you guess that was what I was thinking?" Conrad asked, and slowly raised his eyes to meet Melissa's. No one, even in court, had been able to guess what was going on in his mind. It was one of the reasons he was so successful so adept was he at concealing his emotions and thoughts.

"Habit I guess...the way you were touching it, many have sat there and asked that very question." Melissa said pointedly.

"I see...well I can certainly understand why...it is a unique piece of work." Conrad lowered his eyes again to the intricate pattern he was tracing with his fingertips. He felt an almost uncanny feeling of anger and despair. Mentally shaking himself again he looked at Melissa. He was drawn to her eyes. They seemed familiar somehow but logic was telling him that it was impossible -- he had only just met her. She was staring right back at him puzzled but curious in her expression. He could not explain the feeling of having touched this desk before, and her eyes, it was almost as if... swiftly he looked away.

Melissa was indeed puzzled. It was true that many people had admired her father's desk but none had touched it so familiarly. Shuddering involuntarily she gingerly touched the chain that was around her neck. She recalled the moment when she finally opened the leather pouch. It contained what she thought was the most exquisite piece of jewellery she had ever seen. Each gem had been painstakingly etched with a strange symbol that did not detract from its brilliance. To Melissa they just looked well worn and unique. She fingered the largest gem; a rare shade of green encased in a knot work of silver. She could almost feel it grow warm under her touch.

Conrad looked at Melissa's fingers as they caressed the pendant. Unexpectedly he had the most powerful urge to reach out and grab it! Luckily, Suzy interrupted his thoughts before he made a complete fool of himself.

"Are you sure you two wouldn't like a drink before we start?" she asked looking from one to the other totally oblivious to the strange atmosphere that enveloped the room.

"Hmmm...oh...yes please." Melissa answered her, snatching her hand away from the pendant and looking up to where Suzy was standing.

"Mr Mackenzie, how about you?" Conrad, still shaken at the thought of what he had nearly done, was finding it increasingly more difficult to keep his composure. He coughed politely before he answered.

"No...err...I mean...no thank you" his eyes snapping back to where Melissa's pendant was resting.

Looking back and forth between Conrad and Melissa, Suzy shrugged her shoulders. "Well...I guess that just leaves me then" and she poured herself a large vodka and coke. She took her seat alongside Melissa and they both waited expectantly for Conrad to start.

Picking up his case and laying it on the desk with unusually unsteady hands he waited a moment or two shuffling the papers before he began. Suzy clasped hands with Melissa as Conrad began reading the will.

"Miss Conway...I hope you know that it is with great regret that I am here today and I offer my sincere condolences." Feeling slightly more at ease he continued with his usual opening statement.

"Unfortunately, it is also necessary. You understand that your parents' estate here in Oxford as well as the properties in Scotland and Northern England now revert to you."

Suzy audibly gasped and squeezed Melissa's hand. "Bloody hell!" Slowly releasing her grip she tried to cover up her outburst by blushing furiously. "Shit, sorry Mel...did not mean to interrupt, but...wow...shit...wow!" and she rubbed Melissa's hand furiously.

"Hem...yes quite..." Conrad, sounding very formal and feeling more like himself gave Suzy a very 'solicitor' like look of disgust. Melissa, despite the circumstances, could feel the corner of her mouth start to twitch. Abruptly it went as quickly as it came as Conrad's eyes shifted to where she was.

"As well as the estates there are also some personal effects and documents that have been bequeathed to you. You may or may not know the significance of some that has been left. All I can say is that your inheritance is quite substantial. We have below the London offices a vault, which at this present time is where the some of the items are being stored."

Conrad's voice was steady and hypnotic, Melissa thought, as she sat there listening to, but not entirely hearing, the rest of the will. She began to feel gently comforted by his words and her mind began to drift...she could hear strange voices whispering, getting louder and angrier. Unable to make out the words Melissa drifted further. There was a smell. Hmmm Melissa thought, definitely a sweet floral scent. Something else too...ah...a man's scent...masculine, with traces of...mmm...spice...yes definitely...sweet...now what was the name of it... could it be ginger? The scent made her feel warm and safe, happy in fact. Suddenly a spasm of pain surged through her entire body causing Melissa to clench her fists. Taking a deep breath she tried to steady her trembling body.

"Are you ok?" Suzy, sounding genuinely concerned, started to pour Melissa a drink and tried to thrust it in to her hand. Conrad looked puzzled too. For a moment it looked as though she was in some kind of pain. Melissa opened her eyes and noticed Conrad and Suzy's look of puzzlement and concern.

"It's...ok..." Melissa whispered. Suzy stood with her hands on her hips watching Melissa as she spoke not believing that for an instant. Heedlessly Melissa carried on

"I...probably just need some air" and smiled weakly. Suzy was about to add 'yeah right' when Conrad interrupted.

"Miss Conway...if you are sure you are ok" he said without wanting to sound brusque. "That concludes your mother's will" and he began to shuffle the papers placing them back in to his briefcase. Raising himself from behind the desk he then walked around to the other side. He was almost scared to hold out his hand to Melissa and so kept it at his side.

"I will need you to come to the office Miss Conway...don't worry it's just a formality. I just need you to sign some papers and if you like show you the items in the vault. There is no urgency..." Noticing that Melissa had turned quite pale he added in a much less businesslike manner, "please... Miss Conway... in your own time."

Melissa looked past him and gazed at the portrait of her mother that hung opposite her father's desk. Closing her eyes briefly she took a deep breath before she opened them to look directly at Conrad.

"Yes, thank you, but it's not necessary. I will be there tomorrow." Melissa half whispered closing her eyes once more.

"As I said there is no immediate rush...but if you are sure. I will have everything ready for you. Shall we say about 11 o'clock?"

"Yes, 11 o'clock is fine." Melissa said raising her hand to him. Conrad cautiously and with no choice extended his own hand.

This time, instead of the bolt of emotions he had felt before, there was nothing leaving him feeling almost bereft. Melissa, feeling everything was just too surreal, touched his hand only for the briefest moment. Turning to face Suzy he hastily made his goodbye.

"I'll see myself out." Glancing once more down at Melissa, he added "until tomorrow then, goodbye Miss Conway."

"Tomorrow" she said trying to catch her breath. Melissa waited until she heard the door close and got up.

"Come on Suzy let's go out for a bit." Walking into the hallway she grabbed her jacket. Suzy followed her realising that now they only had each other. As they made their way round the side of the house Suzy caught sight of old Ned in the paddock. "I know," Suzy, said excitedly, "Let's get a couple of horses saddled and head out to our favourite spot".

"Ok why not!" Melissa answered, beginning to feel the need to ride fast and hard with the wind whipping through her hair. Old Ned saw the two girls approaching from the side of the house and tried to put a smile on his aged rugged face. He too felt a deep loss.

Ned had worked for the Conway's since he was a small boy and had watched Melissa grow up to be a fine woman. He often thought of the times she was learning to ride, never minding how often she was thrown from a pony. She just got straight up, brushed herself down and remounted without a word of complaint. She would often stay back to help him, though she knew her mother disapproved. He let out a sigh. Melissa never asked for pity but showed only spirit just as she was doing now.

"Hello Miss Conway, Miss Suzy" Ned rasped, nodding at the two of them. "It's a fine afternoon for a ride". The sun was peaking through a passing cloud and the warm breeze was picking up typical of September. Ned led the two girls into the stable block while sending Tommy along to get the horses ready.

Melissa and Suzy rode like two hellions across the wild open landscape neither one wanting to stop. Melissa slowed Enigma, a magnificent chestnut and so named as he was a difficult colt to break, when they reached the invisible border that divided the neighbouring estates. Suzy reined her less glamorously named charcoal coloured mare called Soot in and came to a halt beside Melissa.

"Its beautiful out here" Suzy said in a whisper. Melissa looked back towards the house, which was far off in the distance.

"Yes" Melissa said, removing a stray lock of hair from her eyes. Turning in her saddle she surveyed the surrounding landscape. "Yes, it is Suzy, it's truly beautiful."

Melissa always felt a deep peacefulness whenever she came to her favourite spot. The landscape stretched as far and wide as the eye could see and was made up of a patchwork of yellows, browns and greens. The contours of the land gently rose and dipped although they were too small to be called hills and glens. Scattered copses made dotted paths between the forestry on the horizon while the river flowed sedately meandering its way through this glorious vista. The setting sun began to turn the sky in to a dance of purples and pinks while lone clouds swept majestically across the sky in time to the tune. The wind that had earlier whipped their hair in to frenzy had softened; allowing the sound of rippling water from the nearby stream to drift over.

Melissa and Suzy both dismounted and led the horses to the stream to drink. Melissa sat down on a group of rocks near the bank and Suzy, as was customary, plopped herself down sitting cross-legged in the shade of the old oak tree. It was so old that some said it had stood for over a century.

"What will you do now you have all this?" asked Suzy, looking up from where she was sitting and making a sweeping gesture with her hand. Melissa, thoughtful for a moment, looked towards the setting sun before she turned to face Suzy.

"There is not much I need to do. To be honest it all pretty much looks after itself. Fairwinds was the only residence, which my parents ran themselves. The other houses are all fully staffed and they look after things. I will probably have to visit the other houses to make sure that all is ok with them. Apart from that I will probably do some travelling... go to some of the places that I've always fancied visiting."

Both girls, each silently lost in their own thoughts, did not notice the horses getting restless or that dusk was beginning to settle around them.

"Hey!" said a male voice. Suzy groaned inwardly as she recognised Adam approaching on his horse waving his hand while shouting out.

"Oh look, there's Adam," Melissa said, as she too recognised the man approaching on horseback. Adam slowed to a halt beside Suzy. Melissa smiled up at him not noticing the look of disdain on Suzy's face at his arrival.

"Hello Adam, have you come to rescue two damsels in distress?"

"If I thought you would need rescuing it would mean a job for life!" he said jesting but looking intently at Melissa.

"Well!" said Melissa "I always thought you were our knight in shining armour!" Suzy very nearly choked.

"I am". he said with an elaborate sweep of his hat. Still not looking in Suzy's direction he carried on. "Which is why I was riding out to invite you over to mine for supper. I only just found out that you had returned. I'm so sorry to hear about your mother." As though he suddenly remembered Suzy sitting there he paused briefly before adding "you can come too if you must."

Suzy gave in to the inevitable while she remounted her horse and reluctantly followed Adam and Melissa. On the way Melissa chuckled to herself. Thinking about the three of them she supposed Adam was a kind of knight in shining armour in his own way. After all he had rescued herself and Suzy on more than one occasion. Looking at Adam a bit more closely she thought he had grown to be quite handsome. He wore his hair unfashionably long as it hung loosely just past his shoulders. The setting sun made his blonde locks look quite pink and again that made Melissa chuckle. Adam was so adverse to the colour pink!

She remembered the time when she was seven and he ten; At one of her parents Christmas balls he had dared her to dress up as a clown and so she dared him to dress up as a doll tying pink ribbons in his hair. As they both went down the stairs into the ballroom everyone started pointing at them while bursting with laughter apart from her mother of course! Thinking it was not that funny she grabbed Adams hand and dragged him back upstairs calling all adults utterly despicable. She realised when she was older that they were mostly laughing at Adam as he had indeed looked every inch like a little girl. 'Hmmm...' he did not look anything like a little girl now though'. He had broad shoulders and a narrow waist and beneath his trousers she could make out his muscular thighs. She checked herself. As handsome as he was Melissa almost thought of him as a brother and was sure he felt the same way as her. After all they had practically grown up together. It must have been at least a couple of years since she had seen him last so she was actually looking forward to catching up with him.

When they reached Langford House Adam dismounted first and helped Melissa leaving Suzy to dismount by herself. Adam linked his arm through Melissa's and walked through the side entrance into the kitchens while Suzy trailed behind them. Temporarily forgetting Adam Suzy thought she was in heaven when she entered the kitchen as the aroma of freshly baked bread and scones instantly filled her nostrils.

"Don't tell me Mrs Betts is still here?" she said as she walked over to the table and not being able to help herself picked up a freshly baked scone and started licking her lips.

"Miss Suzy you haven't changed a bit!" Mrs Betts said as she appeared through the door with a smile on her face. Even though she had worked in Adam's household for more than forty years she had never lost her Cornish accent. "You three sit down and I'll make some tea."

"Well I'm bloody glad for one thing and that is Mrs Betts as these have got to be the ultimate scones in all of scone making history!" Suzy declared holding a scone up in a toast to Mrs Betts.

"Hmmm" said Melissa, "I have to agree with Suzy, Mrs Betts, these are absolutely delicious." Mrs Betts winked at Adam as she placed the teapot on the table. She poured out the tea and handed each of them a cup.

"I'll be off now Master Donell. There's some cold meat left in the fridge along with some cheese. Fresh bread is over there by the stove. Plenty for everyone I would say. Goodbye Miss Melissa, Miss Suzy."

All three said goodbye to Mrs Betts in unison. Melissa got up to get the meats and cheese from the fridge while Adam brought the bread over to the table. The three of them talked and sometimes even laughed late into the evening. Neither Suzy nor Adam gave Melissa any indication of their bitterness towards each other.

Adam, usually so careful around Melissa, could not stop himself from looking at her intently. He thought of all the times they had spent together as children, even when they were in their teens, but mostly he thought of the times she turned to him when she and Suzy got themselves into a scrape. Feeling a little more sombre he now wondered if Melissa could feel anything more for him than just a brotherly figure. He remembered when they were both fifteen sitting in the barn after a morning's ride. Even then he knew she would blossom into the woman who now sat before him. He recalled the scene in his mind when she had sat down and shook her glorious long dark hair as she took off her riding hat. He had so desperately wanted to touch her hair and to feel it through his fingers and at the same time ball it in his fist so she could not escape him. He sat down next to her and reached out to gingerly caress her breast as she lay down nestling into the hay. His inexperience and desperation meant his caress was rough as he tried to fondle her. She had tried to get up, shocked at what he had done, so he pinned her down with his body kissing her clumsily. Melissa had been frightened and bewildered and had started to jerk her body out from under him. Realising he had gone too far he had jumped up and with his back to her apologised profusely, begging forgiveness. Melissa had offered her forgiveness but she had run out of the barn and left him cursing himself. Melissa laughed at something that Suzy said and Adam, brought out of his reverie, moved his gaze to her mouth. Such a sensual mouth; he wanted to taste her lips, grasp her hair as he had wanted to then and pull her to him so he could bruise her mouth with his own. He shook himself. Knowing that she was vulnerable he had to be patient. The pendant she wore around her neck seemed reminiscent of a warning beacon. He had remarked to her earlier how like the colour of her eyes one particular gem was. He sensed it was old and wondered briefly where or from whom she might have got it. He also did not doubt its value, even the smaller gems either side must be valuable in their own right. For as long as he had known her she had always worn it. His mind's eye pictured her naked spread across his bed with only the pendant on. He was almost jealous of it as it lay against her skin tauntingly between her breasts.

He had dreamt many times about feeling her soft skin beneath his own. He wanted to possess her. Wetting his lips in anticipation he knew he would not have to wait long...

For now all he had to do was bide his time and show his support. Looking once more at the pendant he felt the sudden cold chill of jealousy surrounding him mixed with anger so fierce his blood boiled. Outwardly, not one trace of his torment showed on his face.

CHAPTER FOUR

The moonlight teased the room through the tapestry covering the window. He looked longingly at the raven-haired beauty that was watching him from the bed. His gaze slowly swept the entire length of her until his eyes rested on her face. Lips, lush and full, slightly parted in anticipation. Eyes that were unlike any shade of green that he had ever seen. He moved away from the door and over to the fireplace placing the last of the logs on the dying embers. The flames licked the logs tentatively until they played a merry dance. He was careful not to build it too high but just enough so it would last until the small hours of morning. It was a very special night, this night. The raven-haired beauty sighed contentedly as the warmth from the fire reached her. She could not believe that this night could be the last time they would be together. She now realised that she had loved this man since being a wee lass. Even with his back towards her she trembled with expectation in his presence. When he turned from the fire looking directly at her piercing grey eyes smouldered and became a fathomless mist locked with her deep pools of green. She shyly beckoned him to her side. Needing no encouragement he went willingly to her. As he lowered himself on the bed he reached out to remove a stray lock of hair and tuck it behind her ear. She felt her body respond to the feather caress of his fingers against her skin and her eyes fluttered shut.

...He took the green gemstone he had scoured the Highlands for from the pouch concealed behind his back. He turned her around slowly placing the gem over her head letting it rest between her breasts and fastened the leather bond around her neck. Turning her back to face him his lips joined hers in a moment of pent up, pulsating need, emotion so intense he nearly lost control. She felt his raw primitive lust, along with the love he had denied for so long, strip away all the barriers she had erected and fill her with such exquisite passion that she surrendered her heart with a will that matched his...

Passion ebbed and flowed building into a tidal wave. She could taste his desire as he plunged his tongue deep into her mouth. With her crushed to him they fell together on the bed and sank as one into the deep feather filled mattress. He broke away from her momentarily to pull his plaid off from around him stroking her face achingly as he did so. Her breath was shallow and she shook not from fear of what was about to happen but like a butterfly about to be released from its lonely cocoon.

"Och mi love, hoo I hae waited fur this..." he said vehemently. Not taking his eyes away from her he lowered his hand to her breast and slowly caressed her there. The pink bud responded and seemed to swell under his touch. She shuddered uncontrollably as she felt his kisses move lower and the now ripe bud tingled and ached as he tantalisingly licked and suckled it with his mouth.

"Aye...tis true...I hae also suffered the wait..." she replied breathlessly. As each new sensation sweetly tormented her she lost more of her heart to him and was blissfully unaware when he gently pushed her back on the bed.

"Hoo I hae dream'd of ye, lying in mi embrace." He whispered between kisses. As his words reached her she could no longer deny how much she had yearned to hear them from his lips.

His kisses teased and caressed her as his lips and tongue swirled over her skin. Lower he went still whispering words of his love.

"Ye will surrender tae me... only me..." he said, driven with the need to possess her...all of her.

Her breath was deeper now. Her hips responding to the feel of his lips, which left a burning trail in their wake. His tongue found her hot and wet at her centre.... desire overwhelmed him. He knew no other had tasted her sweet nectar and as he kissed her most intimate place he cupped her buttocks and raised her hips to steady her. He drank thirstily, his passion threatening his control. Never had she expected such exquisite torture and was fair certain it was the wickedest of sins. She did not want him to stop. He knew she was reaching the first wave of an explosion; it was unlike anything she had felt before, beyond her wildest imaginings. She tried to twist in his grip and through her ragged breath, groaned loudly as she started to shudder uncontrollably.

He gripped her tighter. Agony and ecstasy took her beyond the place where she laid and she begged him with her body for release. It was far from over he thought as he felt her begin to tremble. The first climax tore violently through her body heady and undulating leaving her gasping for air. He very nearly joined her so intense was the sensation. She tried to still herself but could not control the raging fire he had ignited within her. Burning and feverish she closed her eyes briefly and surrendered to it. Opening them slowly she looked shyly at him, her mouth curving in an instinctive smile.

"Ye are a vision, mi love, yer body was made fur the pleasure only I can give ye"

He began to place gentle kisses on the inside of her thighs and up over her hips working his way slowly up her body to her mouth. Lifting himself up he covered her with his body and placed his hands either side of her. Nudging her legs apart he pushed the tip of his manhood into her wet centre watching her eyes widen in recognition. Entering her slowly he was barely able to control the sweet torture of being enslaved and surrounded by her warmth. Feeling her soften around his shaft he withdrew again once more and unable to control his lust any longer thrust forward and broke through the barrier burying himself deep within her.

Smothering her mouth with his he caught the cry that escaped her lips.

Desire hot and molten surged through his veins. He did not want to hurt her but knew her pain would only be brief. Aching with need to ease his hunger he moved in and out slowly letting her adjust to the feel of him. Their bodies instinctively took over and in that instant she knew she would be bound to him forever. Soaring higher and higher she felt as though she had sprouted angel's wings. Her hands went up around his shoulders and she dug her nails into his back to keep them locked together. As they melted into one their souls reached out linking them forever. Passion and love exploded, desire intensifying with every movement bringing them both to a shattering climax. Trying to control the emotions raging inside of him he gently stroked her face; she closed her eyes briefly and sighed contentedly. His thoughts drifted. His reputation for bedding wenches was well known. Never before had he experienced a feeling of such lust and desire driven by a need to possess which had taken hold of him. Gathering her to him he held her until she fell asleep. Too soon he would be gone. He felt a keen understanding of which he could not explain and an uneasy peace settled around him...

Conrad woke with a start. He had quite a fanciful imagination, which he tried to control, but he could not remember when he last had a dream so vivid. He could even remember the words...he was sure they were...Scottish?

Bewildered he shook his head. He was of Scots blood but he had never dreamed about anything Scottish before. Getting out of bed he padded into the bathroom to splash some cold water over his face. His whole body felt alive and he was aware of a strange tingling feeling. Walking back into the bedroom he looked at the clock beside his bed and saw that it was only three in the morning. Climbing back into bed he waited until tiredness reclaimed him and eventually he fell back into a restless sleep.

He was lying awake when his alarm went off at 7am still picturing the images from his dream. Reaching over to turn it off before it woke the people next door he reluctantly got out of bed and went into the kitchen. Pouring himself a coffee he saw his briefcase lying open from the day before and his thoughts drifted to Miss Conway who he had met the previous day. Feeling unusually hungry this morning he opted for a full cooked breakfast instead of his quick slice of toast with cereal. As he ate he thought back to the events of yesterday. Never had he experienced anything like the mind-blowing barrage of sensations that he had felt when he touched her. Yes...he thought, she was certainly a striking female to behold, but to have felt what he did...there must be something more... Maybe... it had just been too long since he had been with a woman. That is probably it...bloody hell, it must be so severe, I am even dreaming about it...Conrad laughed aloud at his own thoughts. Then more sombrely he tried to think back to the last time he was with a woman and could not actually remember. Picturing her now,he wondered if she was getting herself ready to come to the office. Which reminded him, as he looked at his watch, he was going to be late! Usually when people suffered a loss, such as she had, they put off the signing over of deeds and the other formalities as long as possible. Unless they were greedy of course and in those cases simply could not get there fast enough! He did not think that of Miss Conway as he knew she had requested the reading of the will to be done as late as possible.

He felt a childlike excitement at the thought of seeing her again and tried to dampen the feeling for he knew it was completely inappropriate. Deciding that a quick shower would help he cleansed himself under the piping hot jets and then dried himself vigorously. Feeling refreshed and a little more like himself he put on his best suit and after straightening his tie,drank the last of his coffee not minding that it was now cold. Picking up the documents that he had left out beside his case, he put them back leaving Miss Conway's on top. Grabbing his keys on the way out of his modest apartment, which was located in a quiet suburb of London, he took one last look at himself in the mirror. Feeling excited again he smiled at his reflection and then tried to look stern as a solicitor should do before he headed out the door.

When Conrad reached his office he said a cheery hello to his colleagues as he passed them. Some looked at him in amazement, some even checked their watches in astonishment, while others simply thought he had finally snapped out of his lifelong melancholy. A couple of the ladies, who fetched and carried for the senior partners, giggled to themselves thinking that he had finally found himself a woman. Conrad, of course blissfully unaware of the strange looks and the whispered comments behind his back, continued into his own office that occupied the middle floor. After greeting his secretary he seated himself at his desk and placed his briefcase in front of him. Mrs Collins, flabbergasted at his warm greeting, fled to the coffee machine muttering to herself that she never thought she would see the day that that boy would walk in with a smile on his face. Conrad looked at the time and felt suddenly anxious. Rearranging the documents he had taken out of his case he put them in order and placed them neatly in a pile opposite to where he was sitting. Having second thoughts he decided that he would much rather go through each document individually with Miss Conway and put them back on his side of the desk. Mrs Collins returned and gave him his coffee.

"Will there be anything else, Mr Mackenzie?" Mrs Collins asked as she placed the cup in front of him.

"No, that will be all thank you, Mrs Collins," so she turned and walked back to her own desk. Conrad, looking around his office, suddenly remembered the parcel that had come yesterday. In his haste to go to Oxford he had asked Mrs Collins to leave it on his desk. Tapping his finger on the side of his cup he scanned the tops of the filing cabinets and along the bookshelves that adorned his office. Unable to spot it he called Mrs Collins back into his office just as she went to sit down. "Do you remember the parcel that was delivered to me yesterday, Mrs Collins?"

"Yes, Mr Mackenzie, I left it right over there..." she stopped in mid sentence while pointing to the filing cabinet.

"That is strange..."

"What's strange Mrs Collins?"

"Well, I had the parcel in one hand, while I was putting away some files, and distinctly remember leaving it sitting on top of the cabinet."

"Are you sure it was this cabinet?" he asked while pointing to it. "Could it not have been the one by your desk, Mrs Collins," he added with an arch of his brow. Mrs Collins, having never misplaced anything of Mr Mackenzie's was convinced it must have been the cleaners who had perhaps moved it. She had no other explanation for its sudden disappearance so placing her hands on her hips she replied.

"Yes Mr Mackenzie, quite sure" and returned to her desk thinking she had imagined the smile on his face as he came in this morning. A little taken back by her abruptness he called out to her.

"Don't worry, Mrs Collins, I'm sure it will turn up..." Her response was to get up and close the door that separated them. He knew she was efficient and had never misplaced anything before, but he thought there always was a first time. He felt sure it would surface and hoped it was not anything important that needed his urgent attention.

Turning the cup around slowly in his hand he thought again about the dream he had last night and felt a cold rush of air from behind his chair. Placing the cup back on the desk he swung the chair around thinking the window had come open. When he saw it was closed he looked about him to see where the draft was coming from. That is strange! Still feeling the unnatural chill and not knowing where it was coming from he used his instincts to guide him. Without warning his head began to pound and, awash with dizziness, he closed his eyes. Strange voices that talked all at once whirled inside his mind; he could not distinguish one from another. It was like a giant roar crashing against his eardrums. Conrad tried to block out the noise by covering his ears with his hands. Snapping his eyes open he nearly fell off his chair in his haste to face his desk again. He looked around nervously expecting his office to be full of people. Seeing no one there he slowly let out the breath he was holding and tried to relax. Sinking back into the soft leather his gaze shifted to the documents that sat neatly opposite him. As he toyed with the idea of going through them one more time he dismissed the thought quickly as he was not feeling quite himself.

He whispered Melissa's name softly to himself. She was indeed a rare beauty. Unbidden, images of the raven-haired beauty in his dream sprang to mind once more as though luring him back. He thought how clear the images still were. Normally he could not remember a damn thing about any dream he had had previously and now not only had he dreamt in a language foreign to his own but it was almost plaguing him as he could not get it out of his mind.

Hell... he thought... it was definitely a dream worth remembering. He could picture the half-closed eyes that had peered at him encased in long black lashes. His body moved almost involuntarily trying to gaze deeper into their depths. A cough from the doorway brought him back from his reverie. Looking at Mrs Collins standing there he could not believe he was now having daydreams and smiled rather sheepishly.

"Ah...Miss Collins, has Miss Conway arrived yet?" he said, struggling to cover his embarrassment.

"No Mr Mackenzie, I'm afraid she had to cancel her appointment. She apologised profusely and said she will arrange another appointment when she is feeling more up to it." Conrad felt absurdly disappointed. The elation he had felt so keenly this morning at seeing her suddenly ebbed away.

"Are you feeling well, Mr Mackenzie?" Mrs Collins asked slightly alarmed adding, "You look rather pale."

"Thank you Mrs Collins, I'm fine." After a brief pause, he changed his mind.

"In fact, no, I think you are right. I do not feel all that clever. Could you please reschedule the rest of my appointments? I think I'll go home."

"Yes of course Mr Mackenzie. I will do that right away. I might add a rest will do you some good. You have been working far too hard on those files." Mrs Collins eyed the documents on the desk regarding Miss Conway. Shrugging her shoulders as though this was an everyday occurrence she smiled at him with genuine concern. He had never since she had known him, taken a day off sick. She and went back to her desk to consult his diary. Conrad could not understand what was happening to him. The disappointment he felt was overwhelming. He decided that Mrs Collins was probably right perhaps he had been working too hard in recent years.

CHAPTER FIVE

Melissa replaced the handset next to the bed and stared at it for a moment. She felt so sure she could get through today. Remembering the night before, she smiled fondly to herself. It had been a long time since she and Suzy had a get together with Adam. They laughed and talked until the early hours of the morning and in the end Adam had offered for them to stay over. They had agreed, as it was far too late to wake the stable lad and ready the horses to take them back to Fairwinds. She remembered waking in to one of the guest rooms and dreamily spreading her arms wide in the huge bed while looking at the drapes that adorned the antique bedstead. She knew why Adam had said she could sleep in this room.

As a young girl, she used to sneak into this room, whenever his parents held a party and she and her family were invited. This was her favourite. It was like stepping back in time to an enchanted world. The room had a high ceiling covered in a mural. Fairies danced around the swirling clouds as though in celebration, each one exquisitely hand painted in such detail they looked almost real. The walls were covered from top to bottom, depicting an enchanted kingdom. A fairytale castle took up almost one wall; knights and maidens of a bygone era along with breathtaking landscapes covered the rest. It was truly every little girl's fantasy. The matching furniture was surely priceless; all made of solid cherry wood, engraved with intricate patterns that made you wonder what kind of tools they had used. People used to say it was just a showpiece and no one was allowed to sleep in it. Melissa smiled softly to herself and stared in wonder at the peacefulness and beauty of the room. She felt like she was a young girl again. Gathering up the blankets, she pulled them up higher.

The bed was the grandest she had ever seen, let alone slept in. Even now, she could not quite believe after all these years she had actually slept in it. Raised on its own dais in the centre of the room, you needed to climb three steps just so you could reach it. Thick heavy velvet drapes caressed the four posts at each corner. Each had a silver trim, which glistened in the morning sunshine. It was a sharp contrast to the midnight blue of the velvet. Overhead the drapes all came together in a perfect swirl in the centre, like a huge, silver rose. The drapes fell behind the bedstead in ripples and seductively clung around the bottom of the posts teasing the upper step.

Fluffing up the pillow behind her, she plopped her head back down, and sunk into the overstuffed mattress. Trailing her finger along the top of the sheet, she closed her eyes briefly to savour the feeling and drifted back into an uneasy sleep.

...A young girl of nine was running downhill, as though the wind was lifting her up and carrying her to her destination. She was upset fearing god would never forgive her for trampling over the heather that he had put there to brighten the hillsides. Her heart was beating wildly in time to the thunder made by the group of riders heading toward the castle. For a second she did not think she would make it there in time. Not pausing in her haste, she pushed herself on until she reached the small cottages that lined the road leading to the castle gates. Not caring if she was caught she did not stop until she rounded the back of the last cottage and stopped abruptly to curb her ragged breathing. Gingerly she felt along the side of the wall until she could poke her head round and see the riders as they slowed down to gain entrance to the castle.

"Hey...ye..." A voice bellowed from behind her. She felt the panic begin at her toes and race up her spine until the alarm bells went off inside her head. Just as she was about to make another hasty sprint, she truly did feel the wind beneath her feet as she was lifted from the ground by the rags wrapped around her body. Fear gripped her small form and she tried to fight off the huge pair of hands that were roughly trying to keep hold of her. It was just at that moment the riders approached and all eyes turned to see what was causing the commotion. Slowly she stopped struggling. Hanging limply, she blinked as a hundred pairs of eyes all looked in her direction, penetrating her soul like a thousand knives.

"Mother of god child, whaurever hae ye come frae?" All eyes then shifted to the one whose voice it was.

Proud and stiff sitting atop a white charger the laird's voice shook her out of her numbness and she swallowed audibly as he leapt down to the ground almost gracefully. As he approached, she knew she would probably get a lashing followed by another when her mother found out about this. A young boy, who was half-hidden by the huge man, that had confronted her, stepped out from behind his father. Her eyes widened in disbelief as this giant of a man gently ruffled the boy's hair. Looking from one to the other, she could not help but stare at the boy who in return stared right back. Almost at the same time, both of them squinted to peer more closely at one another, their eyes widening in horror as they realised they were doing the same thing. His father let out a rumble of laughter as he caught the two of them.

"Wha's wi ye lad? Hae ye ne'er seen a wee creature suche as this afore?" Seeing the look of awe on his son's face, he rubbed his chin. "Dinna tell mi, och laddie ye Na be ta'en a liking tae the wee lassie." Opening her mouth to speak, she suddenly remembered the hands that were holding her and she quickly shut it again.

"Hmmm... ye hae fire in yer belly... eh lass?" He tapped the side of his head to bring forth a nagging memory. He was sad for a moment then angry as he recalled the loss of his good friend. Only in his dying breath did he confess the painful truth that he had not sired the wee lass. Revenge had led to his untimely death. For all the lassie's innocence the Laird could not help but feel a slight bitterness towards her.

"Did ye come down frae yonder brae?" he asked, trying to keep the bitterness from his voice and pointing to the hill in the distance. She sensed his tone and mutely nodded in response.

"Tis best ye be getten back." As he turned away from her, the young girl felt the strong hands that still gripped her slip away from her small frame. As her feet touched the ground, she was momentarily immobilised by shock that she hadn't suffered a worse fate. In the space of a heartbeat, she locked and held eyes with the boy, before she sprinted back around the cottages and headed towards home.

The young boy, never having seen the girl before, contemplated silently the strange colour of her eyes. His father remounted with a worried frown, lifting him up with ease and seating him between his powerful thighs. Heading through the gates, the boy knew he would never forget this day...

Melissa blinked herself awake, and felt a little guilty that she had nodded off again. As she hastily climbed out of bed the image of a small boy surfaced in her mind. Automatically she touched the pendant lovingly that lay innocently around her neck Adam and Suzy were already sitting at the kitchen table eating their breakfast when Melissa finally made it downstairs.

"God I'm Starving!" Melissa said, stifling a yawn and sitting down to join them.

"I trust you slept well?" Adam asked as he reached over to pour some more coffee, handing a cup to Melissa.

"Oh...yes...I had to drag myself out of bed." A shy smile played around her lips as she spoke, remembering the feeling of waking up in her favourite room.

"I thought, with my parents no longer here, it wouldn't harm anyone to let you sleep in there. I know it is your favourite."

Looking at her tousled hair and still sleepy expression it was obvious that she had no notion of him entering her room last night. He recalled seeing her lying in the huge canopied bed with just a single sheet covering her body. Every curve was visible through the sheet as she lay on her side. So tempted was he to peel the sheet back to reveal her nakedness, that it took all of the control he possessed to leave the room without disturbing her. Suzy noticed the strange look that had crossed Adam's face. At the mention of his parents, Suzy suppressed a shudder. They had died in a boating accident whilst on holiday two years ago, Adam who was with them managed to escape unharmed. How he escaped when the boat exploded was anyone's guess. The police said it was a tragic accident, but sometimes it made Suzy wonder. Looking at the clock she abruptly got up from the table.

"We need to hurry Melissa, or you'll be late."

"Late for what..?" Adam asked.

"I was supposed to go to the solicitor's office today to sign some papers," Melissa answered while spreading her toast.

"What do you mean? Supposed to...you have to be there in an hour and we still need to get ready!" Suzy said in a fluster.

Melissa laughed at Suzy "It's ok Suzy, I cancelled... After all Mr Mackenzie did say I could take my time."

"Oh..." Suzy said rather disappointedly. "I was quite looking forward to meeting him again." Realising she sounded petulant; she smiled brightly and winked cheekily at Melissa.

"Well you have to admit Melissa; despite his line of work he's rather good looking ...is he not?"

Melissa burst out laughing this time; instinctively knowing what Suzy meant and the two of them giggled like a couple of schoolgirls! Adam at a complete loss as to why they found it so funny interrupted.

"Could you please enlighten me as to why it's so funny?" he asked, trying to smile but not quite succeeding. Melissa, feeling sorry for him, saw his puzzled expression and bringing her laughter under control replied,

"It seems Adam that Suzy here has forgotten all about Richard, who was the love of her life...and is quite taken by Mr Mackenzie."

"Oh Melissa...you make him sound so average!" Suzy said in mock horror. "The man is pure sex! Even his name makes me go all goosepimply! ...Conrad... it just rolls off your tongue...ooh" and she shivered delightedly for emphasis. Melissa, still smiling, shook her head at Suzy's outburst.

"Ok...Ok..." she said holding her hands up in surrender.

Adams expression turned from puzzlement to jealousy as Melissa carried on.

"Well I guess...he is...quite handsome but..." Suzy interrupted her before she could finish her sentence.

"Handsome! The man is a god!" She said flabbergasted.

"Well... I was going to say that there was something a little strange about him...interesting perhaps, but yes... strange."

"Strange? There is nothing at all strange about him...Interesting...most definitely. He is very interesting! Tall dark and handsome does not even do him justice! Ooh...I bet he is over six foot ...and those eyes...so unusual, stormy and dreamy at the same time...I bet that underneath his suit he's got a body to die for!" Suzy only just managed to stop herself from falling off her chair she was sitting that far forward.

Adam sat there listening to Suzy's babbling and began to build a picture of Conrad in his mind, suspicion and resentment twisting his gut. Ok...so what he thought bitterly. He may be dark but I'm blond and everyone knows that blond is better. Tall...pah...I'm most likely taller. Eyes that are 'stormy and dreamy' indeed, probably just plain boring brown. Mine are a brilliant shade of blue. Handsome she said...like a god... she said ...well...god does not exist. He is just a solicitor, common and boring and no doubt leading a boring life...pah. With an icy calm, he pushed all thoughts of Conrad from his mind keeping his expression blank. One thought stubbornly remained of Conrad with Melissa. It taunted him mercilessly.

Melissa's heart unexpectedly missed a beat, lost in her own thoughts of Conrad. Privately contemplating Suzy's words, she remembered his eyes and the soft timbre of his voice. Perhaps she thought, it was the slight accent that had warmed her. She had to admit there was something definitely intriguing about him. Maybe it was just that he had a certain presence... Melissa felt a little silly, but when he had touched her hand, she knew she had not imagined what she had felt...or had she? Admittedly, he was rather good-looking and she could not really fault Suzy for taking a fancy to him. She just was not sure why she did not like that thought very much. Mrs Betts came through the back door letting in a cold gust of wind behind her.

"My...you three have certainly made a meal out of breakfast." She said, surveying the remains left on the table.

"Sorry Mrs Betts, I was ravenous this morning," Melissa answered while Suzy nodded in agreement. Only Adam remained in a stony silence.

"We'd better be on our way," Melissa said looking at Suzy and then Adam. Adam only grunted in reply, excused himself and left the kitchen.

"Well you two ride safely now and don't leave it too long before you visit us again." Mrs Betts said.

Melissa and Suzy both said goodbye and walked back through the house passing down the corridor that housed a few portraits of Adam's ancestors. Suzy could not help but remark on them to Melissa as she looked at each one. At the fourth one Suzy stopped.

"My God...Look at him!" she exclaimed whilst her jaw hit the floor. Smiling Melissa turned to look at the portrait that had so obviously caught Suzy's attention.

"Ah ... lets see, it says here that this was a Laird of the MacDonnell clan." Melissa thought for a moment.

"That is strange..."

"What's strange?" Suzy replied still drooling.

"Well it's just in all the time we have known Adam, he's always called himself Adam Donnell." Melissa said thoughtfully.

"Maybe they just dropped the Mac..." Suzy replied rubbing her temple... she did not like the cold shiver that ran down her spine.

"Yes but why? ...Adam has never mentioned it before."

"Maybe he was not much of a history buff, anyway...just look at the man in the picture, he has quite a handsome face I suppose, a little scary perhaps, but look at all that muscle, his hands... his thighs... ooh and I wonder..." Suzy's thoughts collided while the past caught up with the future. Raising her hand to her temple this time rubbing harder, she knew in that instant she had to keep Melissa away from Adam.

"Suzy!" Melissa exclaimed, "You have just been drooling about Mr Mackenzie" and began to laugh.

"Well I was only wondering if it was true..." in trying to cover up the sudden flash of clarity she had experienced she tripped over the next few words... "you know... about what's underneath!" Suzy replied, tilting her head to one side and looking completely innocent and like the Suzy Melissa had always known. Melissa shrugged her shoulders and with a smile thought that Suzy would never change.

Afterwards Melissa and Suzy made their way out to the stables to ready the horses and go back to Fairwinds. Adam came up behind them and startled Melissa just as she was about to mount.

"Here, let me help you." He clasped her about the waist turning her so she faced him.

"Oh, thanks," she said, not actually minding where his hand was resting. Recalling the man in the portrait, she thought she could see a slight resemblance. Maybe she would ask him about it, over dinner perhaps. Raising her foot to his cupped hands, he lifted her up. Once she was seated, he ran his fingers lightly down her thigh increasing the pressure as he reached her calf. As he adjusted the stirrup, he looked up at her.

"Well they seem secure," he said after he walked around to check the other one.

"Thanks again Adam, It only seems right that I should repay your invitation. Shall we say dinner tonight at Gillespie's?"

Suzy, catching the last bit of Melissa's reply as she mounted her own horse, did not think it was necessary to repay Adam at all. Just as Melissa had seen a resemblance between Adam and the man in the portrait, Suzy thought about what she had felt. Something about the look on his face... she shuddered and did not miss the way Adam had touched Melissa's leg.

"I thought we could get away for a few days, you know, just until you felt ready to sign all that paperwork?" She said as she turned her horse around to face Melissa.

"Yes, I would like that very much" Adam said not taking his eyes away from Melissa and replying as though Suzy hadn't spoken.

"Ok then. Eight thirty and do not be late. A woman hates to be kept waiting..." Melissa laughed softly and smiled at Adam.

Suzy, keeping her thoughts to herself, decided she would have to keep a close eye on the two of them. Melissa seemed unaware of the sinister way Adam moved. The last thing she wanted was for Melissa to become involved with him. She could not let that happen and vowed silently she would do everything she could to prevent it happening. As though Adam had read her mind, he turned to face Suzy with a look of pure hatred. Suzy abruptly turned away from him not wanting to show her fear.

Adam with a smug look on his face stood back and watched them go. He was not worried about Suzy. In fact, he almost laughed, he would soon have Melissa right where he wanted her and Suzy was no match for him. Walking back in to the kitchen he finally let go of his cool composure and went up to his room. Looking at the clock beside his bed, he went to the chest that dominated one wall of his bedroom. Removing a small key from his pocket, he opened one of the drawers. Taking out a manila folder, he placed it gently on top of the chest and closed the draw locking it again securely. Pocketing the small key once more he went over to the wardrobe and took out a clean shirt. As he changed, he glanced again at the clock. He himself had an appointment in London, one he dare not cancel.

CHAPTER SIX

Fashionable old town houses lined the side street that housed the office of Mr Winchester but to all those knew him he went by the name Winchester. Adam checked his watch. Hmmm...I am too damn early he thought as he approached no. 16 and looked around for a suitable bench to sit and wait for a few minutes. Seeing none, he took a deep breath and climbed the stairs to the main door. As he scanned the brass plaque looking for the buzzer to Winchester's office, his eyes focused on the name 'Mackenzie's & Sons'. Just seeing the name reminded him of Suzy's remarks and he cursed under his breath. Just then, the main door opened and a man slightly bigger than he came out in what appeared to be a distinct hurry.

Without glancing at the man who stood in the way, Conrad brushed past him and ran down the steps onto the main walkway. Something prickled Conrad, so he stopped and glanced back at the way he had come. Not seeing anyone or anything that would have caused the reaction, he turned back and carried on towards his apartment.

Adam grunted at the man's back, as he had almost pushed him out of the way, and straightened his tie in a habitual fashion stepping inside as he did so. This was the second time he had come to Winchester's office, just for an instant Adam felt a tinge of fear and gripped the folder in his hand more tightly. Not taking much notice during his first visit, he stood for a moment surveying the lobby. It still had the slight air of a lived in town house as there were portraits lining the walls leading up the staircase. On the far side of the lobby there was an open fire with two leather sofas. A bookcase tucked in to an alcove and traditional wall lamps gave the room a very subdued masculine feel. He wondered briefly if those were the faces of whoever had owned it previously.

Winchester's office was on the third floor so he began to climb the stairs looking at each of the portraits as he passed. One in particular made him stop.

It was a picture of a young woman sat astride a white stallion, revealing her thigh as well as her elegant shoulders in a dove grey dress. Her long dark hair flowed freely down her back and her chin appeared slightly raised. There was a glint in her eyes that devoured the observer and no doubt the artist too he thought. It seemed obvious that the artist, whoever he was, had focused on her magnificently vibrant green eyes, as they drew the observer into the portrait. Adam thought about the contents of his folder as he reached out to touch the painting. Lust stole through him and he snatched his hand back. If a mere painting that resembled her could do that to him, he did not know how much longer he could control the urge to make her his. When he finally reached the top floor, four stories up, he paused to take a deep breath and masked his lustful thoughts. He had to appear entirely calm.

Winchester had a formidable reputation, although on the surface he appeared to be a respectable businessman who mixed with the wealthy and titled. It was just a cover, which cleverly hid his more sadistic nature. He made his money from illegal gambling dens and prostitution. No one knew it was Winchester, who operated the clubs. Unless, you found yourself in trouble, Adam had seen first hand what happened when you did just that.

Six months ago, he went to a club called Annabel's with a group of his old school friends. One of them had heard about the place through their father and described it to the others who insisted they wanted to go see for themselves. It was the kind of place that needed no advertising, as only in certain circles would the name Annabel's be whispered in your ear.

Adam and his four friends found Annabel's tucked away down a narrow side street not far from the Ritz. They were slightly disappointed at the plain looking wooden door with 'Annabel's' scrolled across it in what looked like white chalk. Adam found the buzzer hiding under an overhanging leaf and pressed it firmly. He then put his ear to the door but heard no sound. Feeling a little nervous, they waited to see if anyone answered. Just as they were about to turn away, they heard the door creak open and they all gaped as a beautiful Asian girl opened the door and slowly assessed them from head to foot. Without speaking, she opened the door wider to let them in and led the way down a dark corridor lit only by wall-mounted candles. The chink of glasses, conversation, and soft laughter amidst the spinning of a roulette wheel slowly reached their ears. As the noise became more distinct, the corridor opened up into what must have been a huge underground cellar, which now resembled a cross between a harem and a private casino. Two of his friends headed straight for the wheel and started to place bets. Adam, wanting to relax a little first, went to the bar and ordered a drink and sitting on a bar stool lit up a cigarette, as the other two went to the card tables. The same Asian girl who had let them in approached Adam at the bar. She stared at him for a full minute then walked away without saying a word. She reached an attractive looking blonde who was reclining on one of the sofas and bent her head to whisper something in her ear.

"Be careful of that one Tina, he looks the sort who would like the type of service you provide. Only I think something evil runs deep within him."

"Miomi, but he is so young... just to reassure you though I'll be careful, ok?" Tina smiled brightly then chuckled as she added, "that is if he ever plucks up the courage to ask!" Miomi clucked her tongue and gave Tina a warning look before she turned and walked away, crossing herself as she did so.

Adam began to relax after his third brandy in succession and went to join his two friends who were still playing roulette. Laying down a hundred pounds in exchange for chips he placed his bets and found that lady luck had decided to shine on him. He doubled his money on the first spin and doubled again on the next as a small crowd started to gather around to watch. After two more spins he had doubled up again. His friends urged him to cash in while he was doing so well, but Adam, high on adrenaline and feeling aroused by the two females who caressed his thighs every time he lent forward, did not want to stop. He placed half of his winnings on the table and lost. That was not supposed to happen, not when lady luck was shining on him.

The adrenaline stopped as abruptly as the girl's hands. He looked first at his friends and then at the small group who stood gathered around him. Adam narrowed his eyes and with a slow callous smile that caused several people to take a step back, placed the rest of his chips down on the table. There was a hushed murmur as Adam laid them all on number twenty and he sneered at the ball as it began to circle the wheel as though daring it not to defy him. Everyone stopped breathing and all eyes watched the ball in mute fascination as it circled the wheel not three, not four, not even five, but six times before it fell into number twenty. Adam did not hear the hushed murmurs or witness the stupefied stares of those around him. He only saw and heard the ball spinning tauntingly. A powerful surge of adrenalin coursed through his body as the ball landed in his number and a huge applause shook the room. Still dwelling in his timeless world Adam touched his cock and felt it stiffen beneath his trousers. He felt intoxicatingly dominant and revelled in the crowd's admiration. Feeling a woman's hand caressing his own he looked up at the girl who had now linked her fingers between his.

"Would you like to go somewhere a little more private?" she whispered. Adam could only nod and so she led him away.

They left the room and followed a series of corridors until she stopped outside a door. She reached into a concealed pocket and pulled out a small key. Opening the door wide she led him in to the room and sat him down on the bed. Adam, still hard, never noticed the walls or the sparse furniture. He just took his cock out and started to stroke himself.

"Wouldn't you like me to do that for you?" She purred and removed his hand.

"Is this some kind of freebie?" Adam asked.

"You have won me." She replied softly, while still stroking his cock.

"What do you mean? Are you some sort of prize?" He asked.

"I see you do not know the rules. You do not pay for a girl as such here. You gamble and the more you win the more choice you have in which girl you want."

"So" Adam spat. "You are all I get?" Adam could not disguise the resentment in his voice. He pushed her roughly to the floor and got up.

"Do they think that I would settle for anything less than what I want!" he spat... "Did you see the power I had over the table? No one could have done what I did tonight. And all I get as a reward is you!" The girl tucked his cock back into his trousers and seemed unperturbed at his outburst.

"I see you like power and control...mmm...perhaps even a little rough...yes...yes I can see it in your face; too handsome by far, but you will have to win much more to get a girl who likes it as you do" she said with contempt.

"How much more..?" He growled, as he grabbed her roughly by the elbow lifting her to her feet. She stepped back slightly, fearing the look in his eye.

"Let me see...you will have to speak nicely to Tina. She is the one who likes it rough. Maybe she will take a shine to you and you won't have to win so much." With that, she released his hand from her arm and walked to the door opening it for him to leave. Adam, with his cock still throbbing, left and went back the way he had come until he found himself back in the main room.

He went to the bar and ordered another brandy. As the bartender passed him his drink, Adam leaned forward and asked him to point out Tina. The bartender pointed to a striking blonde whose dress was a deep shade of red that clung to her voluptuous curves.

Tina nodded to the small brunette who had just finished telling her about Adam. She too warned Tina to be careful. He could be dangerous, she had whispered; he had a crazy glint in his eyes and was on some kind of power trip. Tina was intrigued as it was the second time in as many minutes she was alerted to his presence. Looking over to where he stood at the bar, she felt a small thrill of anticipation as she studied him. Yes, she thought, he was young, far younger than herself, but he was certainly gifted with good looks. She wanted him; there was nothing like a young hot-blooded male to make her feel young again, especially one whose tastes were the same as her own.

Disregarding the rules of the club, she casually walked over and brushed the side of Adam as she motioned for the bartender. Adam stared intently at the woman who now stood next to him. She was older than he was but that had never bothered him in the past. She had cool blue eyes with long sooty black lashes, a small nose and well-defined cheekbones. His gaze wandered down her body and he lingered at her breasts as her nipples were protruding through the thin gauze of her dress.

"You like what you see?" Her husky tone sounded so much like Melissa's, that he snapped his eyes back to her face. He began to see her with dark hair. Yes, he thought there were definitely similarities.

"Keep talking," he said in a calm voice that concealed his thoughts. The more she spoke to him the more he thought of Melissa. When he heard her say 'follow me...' he did.

She led him down a different corridor than the one he had been down previously; it felt an eternity before they reached her room. She opened the door and he followed her inside. She slowly removed her dress and clad in just a basque and stockings undressed Adam until he was naked. As she walked over to a set of drawers, she ordered him to lie down on the bed and took out a pair of handcuffs. As she dangled them in front of Adam, she saw that his cock was twitching. He raised his arms so she could cuff him to the bedpost and he lay there defenceless. His excitement grew as he watched her reach for a whip. Gently she ticked him with the whip and then began to caress his balls with it. Her lashings became a little harder as her own excitement grew. He started to buck in time to her lashings and tried to break free of the cuffs

"I have to have you...now!" he roared.

"Ah...so you want to return the favour I see and let your demons come out to play..." she replied and he watched her tongue as it delicately wet her lips.

It was Melissa's mouth that he saw, his breathing became faster and harder and he wanted to crush her lips to his own, to take her roughly as he had always wanted to do. It was no longer Tina that he saw but Melissa and she was his at last... Not only did Tina disregard the club rules, she also failed to heed the two warnings she had received and freed Adam from his shackles. As soon as he was free, he ripped the whip from her hand and in one swift movement; he had her face down on the bed beneath him. Tina felt his strength and it excited her even more until he cuffed her to the bed and began whipping her ruthlessly. Too late, she recalled Miomi's face and the whispered word's of the brunette. Unaware of the thoughts and demons that drove him she begged and pleaded for him to stop, as each lash tore the skin from her body. Adam never heard her cries. Completely at his mercy, she screamed and screamed until she could no longer. She knew that no one would hear. No one would even come. No one would be able to help her. She was alone. Tina's room was the furthest away and screams were commonplace behind her door.

The screams that reverberated in the small room at that night were filled with anguish and pierced your very soul. Adam's lustful demons were unleashed and exercising themselves without restraint. Eventually he threw down the whip, mistaking the blood covering her body as the dress she was wearing earlier. He entered her from behind taking each opening in turn. Tina lay sobbing silently, as she no longer had the strength to scream and began to pray while she still felt semi conscious. The demons drove Adam on and on. All he saw was Melissa begging for more and so he gave more.

Releasing the cuffs from the bed, he turned her onto her back and began to ram into her viciously shouting out Melissa's name with each thrust. Picking up the whip again, he lashed each of her breasts until they resembled her back. Tina felt her life slipping away, every part of her body was abused and torn... she closed her eyes and never opened them again.

Adam spilled his seed into the lifeless body beneath him. Drenched in sweat he rolled off and lay there until his breathing returned to normal. He reached out blindly to touch Melissa in his minds eye, still feeling the exhilaration of claiming her.

Seeing blond hair matted with blood, the elation turned into revulsion. It was not Melissa. Torn between fear and relief, he leaned over the side of the bed and vomited until there was nothing left to bring up. Getting up slowly he looked down at the bed. He thought he was in a nightmare. Where did this body come from? Whom did it belong too? Where was he? Who had done this? Why was he unharmed? As his mind started to unravel the pieces, he vomited again. It was Melissa's fault, damn it. She was begging me and how could I have refused her. He began to wash the blood off his body using the small basin that was in the room. His mind was in chaos. Nothing seemed real. Not daring to look back at the bed, he picked up his clothes, put them on, and let himself out of the room. Gathering his scattered thoughts, he composed his features into the mask, only the outside world saw and stepped into the corridor and made his way back to the centre room. Discreetly he moved towards the opposite corridor that led to the entrance and left without a backward glance.

Now he was here, repaying his debt. Winchester obviously did not take kindly to one of his best girls being murdered and so after gathering information about Adam, he had sent a visitor to deliver a message for them to meet. Believing the law would not be involved due to the club being run illegally Adam felt quite brave the first time he had come here.

As soon as he stepped in to the office, Adam felt the presence of two large louts who then reached out for him and grabbed him tightly. They shoved him, unceremoniously, into an alcove while at the same time, violently pushed him through into a secret room. Before Adam had time to draw breath, he was, viciously chained to the wall and silenced, by having his mouth taped. They stripped him to the waist and whipped him within an inch of his life. In a cold lifeless tone, Winchester informed him that Adam was to make up for lost earnings. With a sinister nod to the two men who had remained in the room. He ripped Adam's trousers from his body and had him raped for his own enjoyment. Adam was then taken away, semi-unconscious and bleeding profusely. Only to be left outside a rear door to a private hospital with a note pinned to him, where no questions were ever asked. It took four months of skin grafts to repair the damage but the scars were still visible. Knowing he had met his match Adam had managed to borrow half of what he owed and was about to show Winchester how he would get the other half.

He entered Winchesters office without knocking. He was expected. He calmly walked over to the desk and took out the documents one by one. The last one was a photo of Melissa, which he placed gently on the top. Winchester looked at the beautiful girl laughing up at him from the photograph, and looked at Adam questioningly.

"She will become my wife." Adam stated. Still Winchester said nothing but his eyes bored into Adam's.

"She has just come into her inheritance," he added with a smirk. Winchester grunted his approval.

"I need time to let her become accustomed to the idea. At present, she is vulnerable and it will not take much to convince her of my feelings. Undoubtedly she will return them." Adam was so confident in his belief that he did not notice the look of perverse amusement on Winchester's face.

"A few months, that is all I require. She has no one else in her life." Adam thought briefly of Suzy and then dismissed her. "No one will stand in my way, she will be mine. Then my debt to you will be repaid." Adam waited patiently for a response.

"One month. That is all. If you have not succeeded, then you know what will happen. An eye for an eye so they say..." With that, Winchester picked up the photo of Melissa, placed it in his draw and dismissed Adam with a curt nod.

CHAPTER SEVEN

Conrad let himself into his apartment and slowly closed the door. Walking into the kitchen, he flicked the coffee machine on and listened to it hissing and spluttering. He was still unsure as to why he felt so disappointed. Reaching for his phone, he started to dial Melissa's number but before he entered the last digit, he slammed the phone down on the table. 'Shit' he said to himself, what had gotten into him he wondered? First, the strange sensations he felt when he touched her and now the bitter disappointment he felt at her cancelling her appointment! Well, he thought, coffee is not going to help, better off with a mug of tea, so he got up, switched the coffee machine off and flicked the kettle on instead. While he waited for the kettle to boil he suddenly thought of the man he encountered as he left the office. The prickly feeling he had earlier when he left work plagued him once more.

He almost laughed when he thought of what his father would say. As stuffy and conservative as he was, he always remarked on Conrad's intuition or the 'sixth sense' as he liked to call it. Conrad admitted to himself that perhaps that is why he had never lost a case whenever he was in court. He knew instinctively whether someone was innocent or guilty. Normally he just put it down to good judgement. Conrad did not truly believe people had a sixth sense; it was all a fluke of nature. Making his tea, he returned to the lounge. Turning the TV on, he sat down. He picked up the remote control and began to idly flick through the channels. A hauntingly beautiful piece of music filled the room and Conrad closed his eyes, settling back in to the sofa.

...The lithe figure slipped unnoticed through the small crowds of people who milled about the courtyard, trading wares and more often than not insults as a result.

As he watched her cat-like movements, he could not help but notice the reason as to why she slipped unnoticed. The people of his village seemed to make way for her. Never had he seen any of his clan shun someone before, and he did not understand why they would shun a young lass. He stood transfixed at the proud way she held her head up and only just caught a glimpse of the sadness in her eyes when she turned back to stare at the group of people she had just passed. As she turned, she noticed the young lad looking at her. Pulling her shawl tighter about her small frame, she headed back towards the outer gate. Not resisting a last look to see if he was still watching her, she practically bolted when she saw he was starting to walk towards her, picking up speed as he did so. So... she thought, he wants tae see wha I'm about, humph.... She felt the first pangs of excitement as she threw her shawl in the air and made a mad dash out of the gate and down towards the burn. Not daring to look behind her to see if he was following, she waded straight in to the burn and tried to keep her balance as she crossed. He stopped short of the bank, amazed that she had never paused. Well, he could not just stand there holding her shawl that he had scooped up from the ground, so he waded in after her. Hearing the soft splash of water as he entered behind her, she smiled instinctively. As she reached the far side, she had to climb up, as the bank was much steeper. Standing up straight, she was just about to sprint up the brae and see how far he would follow her when she heard a louder splash, followed by a curse. Turning around she let out a peel of laughter as she watched him try to right himself in the water. He could not be more than a few years older than herself she thought, but seeing his clothes cling to his body she knew he would grow into a prize male.

He eyed her curiously. Standing on the edge of the bank she looked as fierce and untamed as the landscape around her. The wind in her hair lifted it skyward and her stance was as proud as the mighty warriors he had seen around his Da's table. Their eyes met and locked. The strange feeling he had felt before when he last looked at her from behind his father came back to him now. He knew that there were differences between them, but she had haunted his thoughts from that day. There were none who could match the wild beauty he saw in the vision that stood before him.

He made his way towards her without losing his balance this time, and as he tried to scramble up the bank, she reached out to help him. Her palm was warm but firm and he was reluctant to let it go when he stood upright once more. Despite his hand still being wet, he gripped her tightly dwarfing her small hand in his. For the first time in her life, she felt shy and not quite sure of herself. It was not an everyday occurrence to have the laird's son's hand in your own. Quickly she released him and stepped back. Still feeling conscious of herself, she patted down her wet skirts in a very uncommon ladylike gesture. Watching her, he could not help but be the one to this time let out a peel of laughter, and he fell down cross-legged onto the grass.

"Ye ken ye needn't bother on mi account," he said in between chuckles and watched as a slow smile spread across her face.

"Mayhap ye'd be richt" and she too fell down cross-legged on to the grass opposite him.

For a moment both of them just looked at each other, not quite sure what to say. Then both began to talk at once...

Conrad awoke a few minutes later and realised he must have drifted off to sleep. Sitting upright, he saw the credits rolling on the screen and thought; he must have dozed for a good thirty minutes. He did not know why he kept having dreams of late about Scotland and the strange thing was it was almost as though they were connected. Shrugging his shoulders, he reached instead for his mobile and tapped in the number for the office. Clicking it off as it started to ring he thought that maybe he should just take some time off, possibly even visit the doctor and see if there was anything that would stop him from having these crazy dreams. Perhaps the doctor would think he was crazy; strange things had definitely been happening to him. Conrad burst out laughing. He was getting carried away, but some time off did seem like a good idea. Pressing redial on his mobile, he called the office once more. Mrs Collins friendly voice came down the line.

"Good afternoon, you have reached the offices of Mackenzie & Sons. How may I help you?"

"Hello Mrs Collins, it's only me."

"Hello Mr Mackenzie, I hope you are feeling better?"

"Still a little tired, but maybe you were right, just over-worked like you said."

"I'm glad you have called actually. I wrote it down somewhere...Ah here it is, Miss Conway phoned not long after you left. She sounded in a hurry but said she would call tomorrow to speak with you."

At the mention of her name, thoughts of a young girl crossing a stream came into his mind. Uh oh he thought, maybe the doctor was not such a bad idea. Why it reminded him of Melissa he was not sure.

"Thanks, Mrs Collins...Did she say anything else...?" Conrad could not believe he was getting goose pimples at the mere mention of her name.

"No, that was it I'm afraid. Sorry Mr Mackenzie, someone else is trying to get through, will you be in tomorrow?"

"No that is fine Mrs Collins, and yes I will be in tomorrow." Conrad replaced the telephone and went back into the kitchen, flicking the switch on the kettle as he went past. Making a fresh cup of tea, he returned to the sitting room and picked up his case. Taking out Melissa's file, he made himself comfortable and began flicking through the documents he now knew by heart.

Melissa had come into a substantial inheritance and Conrad wondered briefly what she would do with it all. He picked up the papers and deeds to the estate in Scotland, skimming the page until he found details of its location. The estate covered approximately 80 acres in Inverness-shire, a wild and untamed part of the Highlands. There was something magical about Scotland. When he was younger his father took him there on holiday, not far from the estate that Melissa had inherited. He remembered having felt a strange undercurrent. Even the air seemed different. Conrad loved hearing the old tales about druids and the fae, filling his imagination until he could almost hear them whispering to him. Conrad breathed a sigh of contentment and let his thoughts drift.

He pictured Melissa's estate in his mind. The hills stand majestically, sometimes piercing the clouds that floated by. The sky is crimson as dawn breaks, turning the purple heather on the hills into different shades of pink. The suns reflection makes a path of gold upon the stillness of the midnight blue loch that sparkles like fairy dust, as a soft breeze creates gentle ripples. The only sound to be heard is that of the loch as it ebbs to and fro rolling over the pebbles as it laps the bank rhythmically. A lone Osprey graces the landscape with its presence as it soars over the crops of trees and can sometimes be seen swooping down to catch its morning meal in the water. A baronial style mansion sits proudly on the bank surrounded by trees, shrubs and wildflowers. A sweeping driveway winds its way through the wooded grounds leading up to the entrance. Secluded and peaceful, it is beautiful beyond compare, and as he pictured Melissa standing on the steps as though waiting to greet someone, he turned his perspective around and saw that it was himself.

Amused at where his thoughts had taken him. Conrad contemplated the idea for a moment. A feeling of contentment settled around him, and the same image that came to mind when he spoke to Mrs Collins earlier came as quickly as it went.

CHAPTER EIGHT

Melissa and Suzy raced back to Fairwinds in record time. Suzy very nearly knocked the poor stable lad over in her haste to beat Melissa, as he ran out to take the reins. He had to jump out of the way as her horse reared up and Suzy slid off the horse's rump unceremoniously, landing on the soft earth on her own rear end! Melissa nearly fell off her own horse with laughter watching the scene before her.

"Well I'm glad you found that funny!" Suzy said hobbling over to join Melissa and rubbing her behind.

"I must admit Suzy. It was the look of sheer terror that crossed your face as the horse reared up."

"Yeah, yeah ok, I admit I would've laughed too if it had been you and would have still fell of the bloody horse!"

"Well there you go, either way you still would have ended up on your backside!" Melissa said still with mirth in her voice.

"Thanks for the sympathy!" Suzy said with a smile, Melissa put her arm around her and the two of them walked into the house.

As they went upstairs to Melissa's room Suzy ran ahead just as she used to, opening the door and jumping straight on to the bed. Laughing, Melissa closed the door behind her and then suddenly turning serious asked Suzy about Adam.

"Suzy...?"

"Oh god! What is it? I hate it when you become all serious... Spit it out. You know I'm no good at the advice thing." Suzy held her hand up to Melissa. "Wait, let me make myself comfortable." Leaning back into the bed and plumping the pillows up behind her, she sighed... "Ah that is better."

"Are you sitting comfortably now," Melissa said smiling.

Taking a good look around her, Suzy nodded, "Yep...ready...oh, hang on one minute." Making pretence at fluffing the pillows up once more Melissa interrupted.

"SUZY!"

Chuckling, Suzy put on her most innocent face. "I'm only kidding...go on what's up?"

"It's Adam."

"Hmmm, what about Adam..?" Suzy said, remembering the look Adam gave her when they left. She shuddered involuntarily.

"Well you know..."

"... You are not... NOT... having those thoughts about Adam, are you?" Suzy replied rolling her eyes and dreading Melissa's answer.

"Don't be like that Suzy, I saw a different side to him last night. A more mature Adam I suppose. You have to admit he is very good looking. He even looks similar to that highlander in the portrait you know the one you were drooling over!"

"I certainly was not drooling!" At the look on Melissa's face Suzy summoned a smile, "Ok... maybe I momentarily forgot myself, just a little." Holding her finger and thumb up to demonstrate, she kept the real thoughts about that portrait to herself.

"Melissa, we have known Adam practically all our lives, you especially. I do not understand. Why are you beginning to think of him differently?"

"I don't know Suzy, it's just that so much has happened recently and Adam has always been there for me."

"I've always been there for you too...you're not going to have those feelings for me as well are you?" Suzy said joking around.

"As if! Oh... Suzy... I don't know. I will see how it goes. Anyway, I have always liked him"

Suzy thought back to the time when she had liked Adam not knowing what yet was to come. It was at one of the Christmas balls hosted by the university that she had finally decided to tell Adam how she felt about him. For years she had watched him from afar, ever since Melissa had introduced him to her. At first Suzy was in awe of Adam for he was the 'cream of the crop'. Girl's giggled when he walked past, whispering amongst themselves about his prowess. He was the best looking boy at university and the most popular. Suzy used to think she did not stand a chance. She talked about him non-stop with Melissa asking her all sorts of questions, as she wanted to know everything about him. Melissa used to think it was really sweet and encouraged her eagerness. However, Adam always paid Melissa the most attention and Melissa, at least back then, used to laugh and tell Adam to stop being silly. They were like brother and sister. Melissa never noticed the look on

Adam's face when she used to put him down gently. Suzy did, and it sometimes used to frighten her, as his normally happy expression used to turn sinister. Suzy could never put her finger on why she had mixed feelings. Being half in love with him herself, she almost pitied him even though it was obvious that he was in love with Melissa. So putting on a very revealing dress to look her absolute best she went to the Christmas ball with the full intention of getting Adam to notice her instead.

As soon as she spied him over by the makeshift bar, she took a deep breath and walked over to him, hoping he would just take one look at her, fall in love, and forget all about Melissa. Her dreams or so she thought at the time, was answered when she brushed past his elbow as she approached and he turned around sharply, took one look at her and said 'wow'. Suzy smiled so wide she thought it might ruin her make-up. They chatted all night and Adam did not mention Melissa once. Suzy was in heaven. Towards the end of the evening, Adam asked her if he could escort her back to her room. Hastily she thought of Melissa all tucked up in bed or more likely asleep bent over her books. She had stayed in to do some last minute revision so Suzy suggested they go to Adam's room instead. She thought she saw a flicker of disappointment cross Adam's face but then he suddenly beamed and kissed her on the cheek, saying that was a much better idea. They practically ran all the way to Adam's room and as soon as he had opened the door and let her in he began to rip the dress from her. Suzy was so caught up in Adam's lust and her own feelings of elation and fear that she did not realise he had pushed her on to the bed and spread her legs, not even bothering to undress himself. In the instant recognition of that fact the feeling of fear returned, something was wrong, she knew instinctively this was all wrong. He was kissing her so hard on her mouth and holding her down with the weight of his body that she could not break the kiss to tell him that she was still a virgin and wanted her first time to be all the things she imagined they would be. This was a mistake...as strange voices spun inside of her head she tried to break away... she needed to think and she knew she needed to be as far away from Adam as she could. Adam's only thoughts were of Melissa. He had waited at the bar watching the entrance for Melissa to come through all night, only she never came. He was bitterly disappointed that she had not showed and so kept on drinking, his anger slowly building. When Suzy approached him he used it as the ideal opportunity to ask about Melissa but never got the chance as Suzy babbled on and on about everything but Melissa. It made him more and more angry. Why he had agreed to come here when he was all set to go to Melissa's room he did not know. He had only wanted to see Melissa, but instead he was here, and Suzy was underneath him. It should have been Melissa.

He stopped for an instant breaking the kiss. Suzy opened her mouth to plead for him to stop but all that came out was a scream as Adam thrust into her without warning. Suzy's eyes started to fill with tears, and she tried to fight him off, but he was too strong. Her first time was supposed to be magical or so she thought. A painful, burning and crushing sensation filled Suzy and visions, thoughts and the earlier voices became clearer and louder as the realisation of what she was and what she was here to do, Suzy's screams became cries of despair... Adam who was lost in a bitter, alcohol fuelled rage drove into her mercilessly, driven by thoughts of Melissa letting him down again. He spilled his seed without care and got up from Suzy's shaking and fragile body. Doing his zipper up he then raked his hand through his hair and bent down to retrieve Suzy's dress, throwing it at her. Too mute to say anything Suzy fumbled as she tried to put the dress back on. Unable to do it up completely and where it had been ripped from her body she clumsily held it together with her shaking hands. She fled Adam's room as soon as he opened the door. Not once did he look at her.

As soon as she had run along the passage way and down the steps she found a small alcove and fell into it. She slid down to the floor, her hands covering her face while tears streamed down her cheeks. She did not know how long she had sat there like that but when the tears slowly stopped, she made her way over to the female dorms and headed straight for the shower bock. Feeling bruised and ashamed she scrubbed herself ruthlessly but still could not erase the marks Adam had left on her body and the images from her mind. Hearing footsteps approach close by she looked at her watch. It was six thirty in the morning. Grabbing a robe from the rail she picked up her dress from the floor screwed it into a tight ball and left the safety of the shower block. At the entrance she threw her dress into the bin burying it underneath the existing rubbish. With a false smile she left the block and made her way to the room she shared with Melissa.

She had not told Melissa anything about that night. In fact, Suzy had not told a soul. Ironic really she thought... She had managed to avoid Adam as best she could while at the same time was aware that she needed to watch him and

Adam seemed not to care and made no passing remark or glimpsed at Suzy whenever they did cross paths. Never once did he directly approach her afterwards or apologise. Suzy blamed herself; she should not have gone to the ball specifically to seek Adam out. It was all her fault.

"God Suzy I'm not about to marry the guy, but I think I could see him in a different light!"

"Hmmm... well... we'll leave it at that. Anyway changing the topic and looking at you with that dreamy look on your face makes me think of your solicitor. Now he is defiantly one to get all dewy eyed over."

"You can have him... I mean Adam is probably right and he is just a stuffed shirt underneath all that gloss. Although he's quite nice, he's also my solicitor!"

"I can picture him in a similar portrait to the one we saw. I guarantee he would look pretty good in a kilt...." Suzy winked and got off the bed. Turning around to face Melissa once more, she asked,

"When are you going to go and see him?"

"Well I can't keep putting it off so I will have to go at some point this week. Maybe I will ring again this afternoon and make another appointment for tomorrow. I suppose you'd like to come, so you can drool over him again?" Laughing, she did not even wait for the answer, as she knew Suzy always had a good eye.

"I still can't get over what he said to you about your inheritance. Do you feel up to talking about it some more? We do not have to if you do not want to, but it would be somewhat exciting to go and visit all of them and have a bit of a holiday. You never know you might even decide to take up residence in one of the other houses."

"I don't know about that, but yes we could go and visit them. Like I said before, even though they are all being looked after I suppose I will have to put in an appearance. It will certainly take my mind off things for a while." Still sat on the bed Melissa contemplated all the things she would now have to do and found it a bit daunting to say the least. She remembered the vault Conrad had mentioned and was certainly intrigued. Having a chance to look at what might be in there was making her curious. She wondered what her parents could have owned that would require a vault. While she was thinking about the vault Suzy broke into her thoughts.

"I was thinking ..." Suzy said it in such a way that Melissa automatically knew what was coming next and with a grin she waited for her to carry on.

"You know Conrad er... Mr Mackenzie I mean mentioned the vault that is below his offices."

"Yes..."

"Well aren't you a little curious about what's in there?" There she goes, Melissa thought and wondered if Suzy could read minds!

"Of course I'm curious. I was just thinking about it myself."

"Could I come and have a look with you. I mean actually come in to the vault and see what's in there, dig around and stuff...Can you imagine what might be in there?"

Suzy now had a look of awe all over her face. Still grinning, Melissa could well imagine that Suzy's thoughts were running parallel to her own. She could feel her own excitement begin to bubble but it was mixed with something else but Melissa could not quite understand. It was like a sudden feeling of urgency that would not go away. Fierce whispers whipped around her head and trapped Melissa where she stood. She looked at Suzy and tried to reach out to steady herself but Suzy seemed unaware and continued to look down at the bed while twiddling her hair. It was the same voices only louder that she had heard before when Conrad had read out the will. The voices... she thought, where are they coming from? What is going on?

Melissa felt trapped somewhere in a time she did not know. It was almost as though they were trying to tell her something but she did not know what. As they continued to get louder, Melissa automatically grasped the pendant that hung innocently around her neck and at once felt its heat pierce its way through the myriad of voices that quietened at the warmth. The heat spread itself through her fingers and down her arms making them feel heavy. Melissa, beginning to feel a little frightened, gripped the pendant tighter until her fingers were burning from the intense heat. Suddenly an image of Conrad flashed in her mind and then the heat abated as quickly as it had come, leaving a warm feeling of comfort instead. Thoughts of Conrad drifted in and out of her mind and she sat back on the bed looking at her long unmarked slender fingers the voices were silenced and she felt wrapped in a blanket of peace.

Suzy finally looked up at Melissa and watched in silent fascination at the way Melissa drifted in and out of a trance like state. Unable to take her eyes of her and unable to move from the spot where she was sitting, she too began to feel trapped, but could not open her mouth to speak. Melissa looked like she was in a completely different place and Suzy began to panic. She did not see the pendant around Melissa's neck begin to glow as it was covered by Melissa's hand. The only odd thought that Suzy had at that precise moment was that the pendant was somehow important. For some strange reason it scared Suzy more than being unable to move. Instantly everything in the room shifted and Suzy tried to open her mouth to scream.

Melissa let go of the pendant so quickly the room swung back on its axis and everything was once again how it had been. The two of them just stared at one another. It was a few moments before either one took a gulp of air. Suzy, regaining her senses quicker than Melissa, was the first to speak.

"BLOODY HOLY SHIT! Melissa. TELL me, WHAT THE HELL just happened?"

Melissa did not have a clue, and still felt as though she was somewhere between two worlds. All she could do was sit and stare at Suzy with the most incomprehensible look upon her face.

"No don't even answer that question. Einstein would have to answer it and he is dead! That was too bloody mind bending...blowing, call it what you want." Still unable to put her thoughts into speech Melissa let Suzy carry on.

"That was the most weird, surreal, bloody boggling thing, I have ever experienced. Shit, sorry for swearing Melissa, but I just cannot bloody believe what just happened. I mean I do not even know what just happened. All I know is that one-minute we were having a conversation and the next, holy hell breaks loose. It's too weird." Suzy prayed that Melissa would believe her and crossed her fingers.

At Suzy's absurdly placed apology Melissa began to come back from wherever she had been. While Suzy sat and continued to wait for a response. Eventually Melissa was able to spit out a sentence.

"Don't apologise Suzy. It's what I love about you." She smiled and added, "you only said out loud what I was thinking and I could not even manage a whisper let alone speak. To be honest I do not have a clue about what just happened or why it happened. I could not even begin to try and understand what just happened let alone what prompted it. Mind blowing it was though... all I can remember is that just before everything got a bit weird we were talking about my inheritance and..."

"The VAULT!" Suzy practically jumped when she said it. "That is it...Do you think it has something to do with what we were talking about just before it all went crazy?"

"The vault.... yes it could be... although I don't know if talking about the vault exactly caused what happened to happen. I mean I've said it again and so have you." Suzy looked suddenly crestfallen, then smiled.

"It might have been because we were thinking about it at the same time. Stranger things have happened."

"No... you know I don't believe in any of that." Before Suzy could look crestfallen again Melissa continued.

"Although something had to have triggered it off I'm just not sure what. Why don't we try to see if it happens again?" Suzy, was a bit apprehensive, and was not that keen on the idea.

"Do you think we should tell each other what we are going to think about?" She asked Melissa.

"We did not last time, so there's no reason to this time. We'll have to try and think of the same thing without telling each other. It would be cheating otherwise."

"Oh come on Melissa, just a little hint..." Suzy's smile was infectious and with a smile of her own Melissa replied,

"No! It might not work." Melissa did not believe for one minute it would work, but was willing to try anyway.

"You don't know that, after all we were both talking about the vault before we were thinking about it along with your inheritance."

"Yeah I know, but somehow I don't think that was all it took. Listen, why don't we just both think about what we have done in the last twenty-four hours and see if we manage to think of the same thing at the same time again. Ok?" Suzy's reply was not as sure as Melissa's.

"Ok..."

"Ready...we'll do it after a count of three...two...one..."

"Wait..." Suzy interrupted. Melissa rolled her eyes... "Do you think I should sit in exactly the same way?"

"What!" Melissa could not help but laugh.

"Well you know, re-enact everything we did before it happened.... I'm being serious Melissa, so don't look at me like that with your, oh so huge, round eyes rolling around like marbles!"

"Oh Suzy, if it will make you feel better then yes we will try and do everything that we did before."

"Oh and could we talk about Mr Mackenzie...Conrad...again too...?" Suzy asked, rolling her eyes to match Melissa's while smiling sweetly.

"Oh alright" Melissa said chuckling "If it will make you feel better then yes we can talk about him too... THEN we will just think and see if it happens again."

"Are you scared?" Suzy asked Melissa, trying to be serious for a minute. Melissa reached for Suzy's hand and grasped it tightly in reassurance.

"Yes I am scared. Who would want to go through that again...willingly? I mean...knowing what is actually going to happen and still doing it anyway."

"Well, there are two..." Suzy said and smiled "There is just one more thing though. It's quite weird actually."

"What? Spit it out" Melissa said as she rubbed her hands together as though they were cold.

"I was thinking of your pendant, it seemed important."

"It's just a pendant Suzy." Melissa stated.

"Yes, you're right." Suzy looked down at the pendant around Melissa's neck, which sat there innocently, secretly confident that it had a greater importance than either of them could have imagined. Then they started to repeat their earlier conversation. At the agreed time they stopped talking and just sat staring at each other, wondering if they were thinking the same things at the same time. Both were holding their breath and let it out simultaneously, bursting into a fit of laughter.

"I can't believe we actually tried to do that!" Suzy spluttered between giggles.

"No, me neither!" Melissa answered.

It took some time before they stopped laughing long enough for them to look at each other again. When they were finally able to talk Suzy said.

"Hmmm...well I guess that did not work..."

"Nope... It did not work, maybe we both imagined it?" Melissa said, not really believing that what had happened had anything to do with imagination. After all Suzy had experienced the same thing, hadn't she? Suzy contemplated Melissa silently. No... she thought...it was not our imaginations.

CHAPTER NINE

As dawn arose the sky looked almost ethereal. Pale orange streaks, punctuated by different shades of red from palest pink to the glowing yellow of the sun, peeked through a dusky blue sky, shaking off the last remnants of the night before. It was certainly a wondrous sight to behold, Maura sighed wistfully. Today was her sixteenth birthday although she did not really expect it to be any different from any other day. So far all her birthdays had gone unnoticed apart from one small gift each year from her mother. Humph... she thought, and she blew the wisps of hair out of her eyes, which had escaped the long dark braid that hung loosely down her back very nearly reaching her waist. Well she would just have to find out later for her mother barely rose before noon due to the strange illness that was making her mother weak. Not wanting to dwell overly on her mother she looked up at the sky.

This was her favourite time of day. Shifting her position so she could bring her knees up to her chest she sighed dreamily. Picking a long overgrown blade of grass, she twirled it mindlessly between her fingers wondering what her mother could have possibly obtained for her this year. It never ceased to amaze her where she found the strange gemstones that had now become a collection of sorts. Growing up on the outskirts of the village, and well away from the castle, she thought her mother possessed some kind of magic as she never went anywhere and no one from the village dared come here. Humph... she thought again. It had not bothered her until now... now that her mother was close to death.

Would the villagers still leave her in peace? She very much doubted it. Although the Laird had let them live here in reasonable peace he was not going to be around forever either. Well, she thought, she would just have to face that when it happened, just like everything else she had had to face up to now. All the cruel taunting she had endured as a wee lass had hardened her on the outside but that wee lass still remained tucked securely deep inside and was never coming out. Only her mother saw through the façade and worried endlessly what would happen to her daughter when it was her time to go. She hated the pitying looks they always cast in her direction whenever she ventured into the village.

Curiosity had gotten her into more scrapes in the village than she could count. At least she could count, probably half the village could not she thought verily. Maybe she was the only child who ran barefoot, dressed in little more than rags, her face always smeared in dirt, but that is all they saw. No one befriended her...except perhaps one... When she was at home with her mother, she learnt the letters that enabled her to read and the numbers that enabled her to count. As she got older and her thirst for knowledge increased so did her understanding of languages.

Her mother, who was born and raised in England, was a distant cousin to Queen Elizabeth the first. She barely escaped with her life when she met and married her Da in secret. Sighing heavily, she thought of all her mother had gone through in her short life. Her mother had to keep her knowledge of learning a secret from the rest of the villager's, as they would have scorned her for being a Sassenach witch. Not only were they a suspicious lot some of them held a deep hatred for anything English. Only her father and the laird knew, as her father was one of the lairds most trusted guards.

Twas the only reason her mother was tolerated, that was until his sudden death in a clan feud against the MacDonnell's. Since then they spent most of their time pouring over books her father had managed to obtain learning about different places and languages Maura became well versed in Latin and French and even learned some Greek.

Maura now wondered why it was that a few women had come to visit her mother recently, staying only a short while, but long enough for Maura to notice and question her. Her mother would just say that they knew her time was near and came to pay their last respects. More likely looking at what they could plunder, Maura thought harshly, feeling the twinges of anger spread through her veins. Most of them had never even looked across at the burn and up the brae, towards her home, much less actually visit. Lying down on the grass, she inhaled the sweet smell of heather that bloomed nearby. The sun had now risen and was teasing a smile from her face with its warmth. Slowly she felt her body respond to the sun's caressing rays and the anger abated leaving her mind to wander freely once more. In particular, she thought of one woman who visited her mother a sennicht ago. Dressed head to foot in black she wore an unusual second skirt tied about her waist in the brightest colours Maura had even seen. As the woman neared her mother, Maura could swear she heard the softest tinkling of charms in time to the sway of her skirts.

Maura had heard of 'Gypsies' - a group of people that travelled from place to place making their home wherever they chose to stop and rest for a while. Sometimes they were welcomed, more often than not, they were regarded suspiciously, even by the Scots. Was this woman one of them? Nay she thought, probably just assumed their dress as judging by the wrinkles on her face she must have been over three score. It was a well-known fact that they banded together, never separating and never settling in one place to live to that auld age. What if Maura was wrong..? That question just raised more questions and only her Mother would have the answers. Maura remembered that morn as though it was yester'. Her mother sat in her favourite chair, wrapped up in a scrap of worn, threadbare plaid just outside the door to their small croft when the woman approached. Maura, who had been washing herself in the burn, had just returned and as she rounded the small croft she stopped abruptly at the sight of the woman in the fancy skirt. She stared in helpless fascination, holding her breath as she watched the sight before her. Leaning forward slightly, she tried to hear what the woman was saying to her mother, nearly toppling over in the process. Letting out her breath, she looked heavenwards-thanking god that neither her mother or the strange woman had seen or heard her. The woman spoke in raspy tones that sounded strange to Maura's ears.

"Nice morn' is it not?" the woman said with a nod in her mothers direction.

"Aye, that it is Brietta...it's been several moons since you last came, it is good to see you again."

Maura's eyes widened with disbelief... It was obvious that her mother knew her, but how..?

"You know I always come when the wee lass has grown in age another year...I have for Maura the stone you wanted for her." The woman held out a small pouch and placed it gently in her mother's hands."

Maura automatically reached for her own pouch which contained small precious stones, given to her over the years and almost wanted to burst forth and confront the woman and her mother. Why was it she had never met this woman? Why had her mother ne'er mentioned her before? Maura's head was sore from so many questions. In disbelief and amazement, she turned and headed back to the burn to cool her brow, deciding that this eve she would demand her mother answer her questions.

Maura's remembering stopped as a shadow passed over her while she lay on the grass. Not sensing any danger, she continued to lay there with her eyes closed, willing the cloud that she assumed to be passing over the sun to hurry. It was only when she heard the soft highland burr of a male voice, that she opened her eyes, slowly glimpsing, the tall strapping highlander that stood over her. Tingling from head to foot she managed to frown up at him to conceal the sensations humming through her body.

Ciar smiled down at her. The impact of his smile did things to her that she could not even put into words. He was dangerous, dark and had more brawn than surely god would have granted just one man. A purely sexual heat radiated from every pore and his legendary skills as a lover, were much discussed amongst the village wenches. Maura was not the only lass who suffered the same sensations brought on by Ciar's smile. Nearly every woman in the village felt like the most beautiful woman in all of Scotia, when he graced one of his smiles upon them. They would drop whatever they were doing and run to do his bidding. Ciar Mackenzie was a giant of a man. A man, whom other men openly respected but also feared and not just on the battlefield, but whenever he came within a short distance of their womenfolk,.

"I hae something for ye lass..." Ciar said and pulled a rather delicate bloom of heather from behind his back holding it out to her.

Maura sat upright and held out her hand to take the heather from him. Bringing it to her nose, she inhaled the sweet smell and a smile almost touched her lips. Tossing them casually to one side she peered up at Ciar with a slight scowl on her face.

"What boon d' ye ask of me now...if it's what I'm nae wanting to be thinking, they'll serve you better given tae one of the wenches.

"Tis nae boon I ask of ye... simply a gift. Tis just mair sportsum tae see what you would dae wi them, as tae knowing what a wench would dae" Ciar replied with mirth.

Ever since her eyes had held him captive as a wee lad, when many moons ago his father had came across her in the village, he had been fascinated by Maura, growing up he sometimes used to follow her whenever he could escape the watchful eyes of the guards. As the years went by he became privy to the whispers that surrounded Maura and her mother. Some of the villagers said she was a 'wee deevil' born of a MacDonnell's Satan's seed, their mouths trembling from merely saying the name MacDonnell. Others shunned her just because she was born to a Sassenach and feared she would put an evil pox on their village. They were a superstitious lot as were nearly all Highlander's. Some would even fear their own shadow he did not doubt. Ciar feared nothing and no one. He paid no heed to the whispers. In fact it made Maura the most tempting and alluring female in the Highlands.

"Ye know I dinnna care for that expression on ye face. Why ye be troubling me on this fine day?" Maura said while trying to shield her eyes from the sun.

"Och lass, I hae nae expression on my face as well ye know. Tis just the pleasure o' seeing ye lying down surrounded by the deepest purple heather in this them hills, warming ye bonnie face in the sun."

Maura, feeling stunned at the fluttering deep in her belly she felt at his words, rearranged her skirts as she sat up. For the first time in her life she was speechless. Ciar had to bite his lower lip to keep himself from grinning. Never had he seen Maura struggling for words, not even when they exchanged friendly banter. Her wit and quickness of mind matched his own. Hmmm...he thought mayhap now she was blossoming she was not as resistant to his charms as she liked to think. Before she had the chance to think of something biting to make him go away he sat down beside her. Maura's heart was now pounding loudly inside her ribcage. Thinking he might be able to hear it she crossed her arms in front of her and managed to look as though his words had had no effect. Shifting uncomfortably, she turned slightly away from him. In truth, Maura for the first time in her life really did not know what to say. Never had he caught her in a rare moment of un-guardedness. She was all at once confused and frightened. Something else she was unaccustomed with, growing up as she had, fear was a weakness and she learned at a young age to hide it.

Ciar was the only one from the village that had befriended her. Oh she'd led him a merry dance and made it near impossible at times, but he kept his vigil. Never once had he given up, so stubborn was he. Over the years, she had actually grown to respect him. In time, she had softened a little towards him enough to speak to him on occasion, which of late, became more and more often. Despite this, she remained slightly wary never completely trusting that golden smile he always seemed to have pasted on his handsome face. Her loneliness though had harboured his company and craved his words as much as her distrust repelled it. Ciar wondered what it was she was thinking even though she had turned slightly away from him. He could still see her profile, the way she knitted her eyebrows together and the way she twirled her fingers about her skirt. He knew something was burdening her. Concerned, he was just about to say something when she turned sharply and looked him in the eye.

"Yer words mean now't...ye'd be wise tae use them on someone else." She swallowed the lie that had passed her lips and hoped to god, in penance, he would not rain a thousand hailstones down on her head. Ciar unfazed by her outburst knew she' had lied but was starting to enjoy her discomfort. Ne'er had he seen her so affected by his presence?

"Och...tis that the way of it then, wha bothers ye lass...normally ye would reply with a wit as good as mine." Ciar softened his expression and Maura for a moment saw he was being genuinely concerned.

"Tis my ma...she's no long tae gae and women from the village hae been tae see her." Ciar saw her puzzled frown as she spoke and raised an eyebrow in genuine surprise.

"Women from the village ye say?"

"Aye...ne'er hae they troubled themsels before. Tis likely they only come just tae see wha they can take when mi ma goes." Maura clenched her fists at her sides as she spoke and Ciar, not wishing to say she was mayhap right, knew that once her mother had gone Maura would lose what little possessions she had and the clan would banish her. He gazed intently at Maura pausing for just a second as his eyes roamed over her beautiful face, flushed with the warmth of the sun and unable to hide her fiery nature. Her eyes held his, glittering, with unspoken courage and defiance. Vowing softly he swore to protect her. As soon as he had muttered the oath a great storm of emotions was unleashed and in barely a whisper, words he'd only ever been careless with suddenly filled him with a possessiveness he'd never felt before.

"I'm truly sorry lass, tae hear about yer ma. I'm sure the women were just paying thair respects..." Ciar filled now with an emotion he could not name watched as Maura fiddled with her skirts and pulled out a small pouch. He saw a shadow of a smile pass her lips as she took out its contents. Fascinated he leaned in closer.

"Och lass, they'd be bonnie stones..." Ciar was touched that Maura had shown him what must be her only possessions. He even thought some could be sold for coin if she were ever to need it. As she held her palm up to him, he could not help but pick one up and roll it between his fingers. Holding it up sunlight poured though its facets causing an array of colours. A crystal he thought, not polished but rough, quite rare in these parts especially as it was almost clear. He put it back picking up another one and again holding it up. This one did exactly the same but looked nothing like a crystal. Not one of them was bigger than a pea and he wondered at their beauty and from where Maura would have got such a gift as these. She studied Ciar as he lifted the tiny crystals up to the sky and watched him smile in awe as a rainbow of colours surrounded him.

Feeling a deep peacefulness, she sighed dreamily, still not quite believing he was actually sitting right next to her. So close in fact, that his scent was doing strange things to her blossoming womanhood. Ciar reached for the pouch with one hand while his other scooped up the crystals from her palm. As his fingertips brushed against her skin a fierce tremor of desire engulfed him. Maura sat dumbstruck as she felt the waves of raw hunger wash over her. Open mouthed she snatched her hand away less it get burnt. At the loss of contact Ciar, shocked and amazed by what he had just felt, hastily dropped the pouch on the grass and jumped to his feet. Confused by his actions Maura did not know if he was angry or disgusted at touching her. Gently she rubbed the spot where his fingers had been just a moment ago, feeling confused and frightened at what she thought she felt when he touched her. She gathered up the stones that had fallen to the ground forcefully putting them away. Looking at him for some kind of sign that he was not disgusted she cursed herself for being a fool. Surely the laird's son would dare not have anything more to do with her than to taunt and provoke her, thinking of it as now't but a game.

Standing up she quickly scouted the ground, less she forgot one of her precious stones and before the tears of shame and hurt could surface. Turned and ran back to her home. Ciar, still too stunned by what he had just experienced, cursed himself for saying nothing of what he had felt. He did not miss the near tearful expression on Maura's face as she fled. Feeling a complete fool, he'd known the instant she fled she'd think he regretted touching her and was now no doubt feeling a deep sense of shame that she had let him. Uttering a stream of oaths, he then made a second vow that he would ne'er cause her to feel shame again.

In a small croft, which stood amid the wild forest that lay on the edge of the Mackenzie's land at least a half a days ride from Maura's own home, sat Brietta. While humming an ancient melody she never once looked away from the flames that seemed to dance in accompaniment, as they licked the blackened log in the fire. When she came to a stop, she grunted with satisfaction...closing her eyes briefly she rose from her chair. When she opened them again she looked across to the windowpane at her long time companion. A pair of almond shaped amber eyes stared back unflinching. A soft purr punctuated the silence in the croft and Brietta whispered 'so...ye ken tae then, my wee feline friend...' With that the cat jumped from the pane and graciously walked over to Brietta, wrapping itself around her legs. Brietta looked sad for a moment at what her vision had shown her, but then her face lit up. Sighing softly, she waggled a finger at her friend. "Tis a fine and fragile thing they'd be sharing..." Chuckling to herself she added "they'd not even be knowing it yet...Maura is a stubborn, wild, wee lassie and Ciar, the Laird's only son...och tis going tae be a battle of wills betwixt those two. That I've no doubt my wee friend..."

As quickly as the moment of joy enveloped her, she shivered as she thought back to that day long ago. She had taken a huge risk in being here in this realm, but until she was certain she had vowed he could not be allowed to win.

CHAPTER TEN

Adam returned home from his appointment with Winchester, his anger barely concealed beneath his cool exterior. Without acknowledging the butler as he entered, he went directly to his room on the second floor. Once inside he approached the large chest that adorned one side of the room and swept everything off the top with one movement of his hand. Hearing the crash of ornaments and a once favoured lamp as they hit the well-polished floorboards, Adam let out a curse. Making no effort to clean up the mess he went instead to sit on his bed. The rage he felt coiled itself around his very soul. Resting his head in his hands he shook his head several times torn between the injustice of his situation and the little time he had left in which to make Melissa his.

If they hadn't insulted him by offering that pathetic girl to stroke his cock, he wouldn't have gone back into the main room to be taken in by the stupid bitch in the red dress. She asked for it... Yes, she definitely asked for it... The more he thought about it the more he convinced himself he was blameless. He would not have done it otherwise... would he? All he could think of was Melissa...it was her...she was there with him...it was her face that he saw, begging him for more... Melissa... ah Melissa. No! His mind screamed. Melissa had tried to stop him... did not she? She wanted to save him from the demons that consumed him, not feed them. "No! No!" he shouted aloud. Melissa was good. She was pure...was not she? She would be his at last and her inheritance would help save him. The rage slowly subsided as his thoughts focused on Melissa. He knew that he had to act quickly. He could not take any chances. Nothing and no one could stop him. Not Suzy... she was a weak female, definitely not Suzy "Pah..." he spat. She was nothing. Winchester. ...Ah Winchester... he silently cursed. A slow menacing smile spread across his face until his features looked unnatural. You will be a worthy adversary but you will lose, as I will not let you beat me again. Once you may have had your fun. Next time it will be my turn. His thoughts of revenge ravaged his mind until he suddenly looked at the clock beside his bed. With what could be mistaken for a genuine smile, Adam got off the bed and called his valet to his room. It was time to get ready for dinner. Tonight the game will begin.

After their experiment, Melissa and Suzy decided to go downstairs to the lounge and watch a movie. When it had finished Melissa burst out,

"Oh god! Look at the time, it's nearly five o'clock! We need to get ready for dinner."

Suzy, who had conveniently forgotten all about dinner, tensed. After being in Adam's company yesterday, she did not know if she could go through it again.

"Do we really have to go? I mean to dinner with Adam. Why don't we just grab something light to eat here."

"Well yes we have to go. I asked Adam and I can't just back out at the last minute can I?" Melissa felt a little annoyed that Suzy did not want Adam to be there. "I could go on my own if you are not that hungry."

Suzy did not want Melissa anywhere near Adam, especially on her own, if she could help it. So reluctantly, she agreed to go. As the two of them made their way back to their bedrooms to get ready, Melissa went to the phone and made a reservation at Gillespie's for eight thirty.

Opening her wardrobe doors wide, Melissa pulled out several items of clothing discarding them one by one on the bed after she had held them up against her. Normally she would go straight to the wardrobe and pick out an outfit straight away. Tonight was a different story, nothing seemed right. She felt a little nervous about going to dinner with Adam as she was starting to think differently about him. Of course they'd had the odd lunch or dinner before now, but she had felt a fluttering in her stomach every time she sneaked a look at him the previous evening. When he helped her mount her horse she remembered the tingling feeling she got as he ran his fingers slowly down her thigh. She felt a shiver now just thinking about it. Up until now, she had always thought of him as a brother, but she had noticed a change in him. He was certainly better looking than she remembered and his quick wit made her laugh throughout the evening. He was charming and polite and not the over eager boy who sometimes sulked when he could not get his own way. In fact, she thought he had obviously grown up quite a bit and had turned out quite nicely. She could not help but notice his strong forearms as he gripped her waist and his muscular thighs in his tight trousers. Melissa wet her lips...yes...she thought I am definitely looking forward to this evening. Finally taking out a silk fitted shirt in dove grey and a black pencil skirt, she put them on and went over to the dresser to apply her make-up and arrange her hair. Melissa wanted to look appealing but subtly so.

Suzy was also making a pile of clothing on her bed, not from being unsure about what to wear, but from the prospect of dinner with both Adam and Melissa. Suzy knew she could not just blurt out what Adam had done to her all those years ago. Or could she tell Melissa about the visions and whispers that had come to her at that time, as she was still trying to work out what the meaning of it all was. So instead she tried to think of ways to get Melissa away from Adam but was not quite sure how she could deter Melissa. Why it was now that Melissa seemed keen on Adam Suzy did not know either. Selecting a plain dress in a navy blue Suzy at least thought she could melt into the background. It was not as though Adam would take any notice of her anyhow. He had already shown that. Suzy wanted to be there for Melissa and do what she could. Despite knowing she had a role to play in their lives the full extent of which remained unclear. Suzy had just finished putting her hair into a clasp when Melissa knocked on her door calling out to see if she was ready. Suzy took one last look in the mirror and taking a deep breath yelled "just coming" in reply. She had been through worse than this she thought, so summoning her strength she practised her usually bright smile and hoped it would get her through this evening.

Downstairs Melissa was just doing a last minute check in the mirror before she rang for a taxi to take them to Gillespie's, Suzy found Melissa in the hall just as she put the phone down.

"Suzy, I've never seen you in anything so...er...plain." Melissa could not help but notice.

"Ah...well...um...I did not really bring anything glitzy as I did not think we would be going out much. You know I thought we would be eating in mostly," Suzy replied.

"It still looks nice though. I did not mean it the way it came out." Melissa said and smiled warmly.

"Oh its ok" Suzy replied with a smile "Its normally me who is the tactless one." A small blush appeared on Melissa's cheeks.

"Sorry Suzy I..." Melissa was about to apologise when Suzy rushed on.

"You look absolutely gorgeous as always!" Suzy realised in that instant that Melissa had obviously gone to a lot of trouble in getting ready. It was the first time in the last few days that she had seen Melissa look genuinely happy and excited.

The taxi bibbed outside to announce its arrival and Suzy reluctantly followed Melissa out of the door. Once they reached Gillespie's Melissa paid the taxi driver and the two of them made their way into the restaurant. Just as the waiter had shown them to their table, Melissa spied Adam at the entrance and waved him over. Taking his place opposite Melissa he remarked how beautiful she looked and Melissa gave him a radiant smile. Suzy quickly picked up the menu and tried to hide the look of horror on her face at seeing

Adam and Melissa in an intimate moment. "I think we should order some wine." Suzy said into the menu.

"Yes, you're right." Melissa replied, and a waiter magically appeared at her side. When the waiter returned with the wine he poured out three glasses and left again with their order.

"Here's to you." Adam held up his glass to Melissa. "The most beautiful woman I know." Melissa laughed softly but could not help but blush slightly. Suzy sat in silence and wanted nothing more than to leave straight away. She did not know how long she could endure listening to Adam's compliments and watching Melissa's knowing smiles. Feeling queasy, she excused herself from the table. It was not as though they would notice, she thought. While Suzy was gone, Melissa, warmed by the wine and Adam's compliments, considered what she felt for Adam. She admitted to herself that she actually really liked him and began asking him questions, forgetting all about Suzy's absence.

"Did you find it difficult when you lost your own parent's?" Melissa suddenly wanted to know. Adam calmly placed his glass back on the table and looked at Melissa for a moment before answering. Briefly he wondered if she was suspicious of his parent's death as so many others were. But seeing a genuine look on Melissa's face he decided that she was most likely being sincere and then argued with himself. Of course, she would be sincere... She is not suspicious - she does not listen to gossip, and is good and pure. He sighed contentedly...this would be too easy...he thought. Melissa, mistaking his sigh for one of heaviness, watched Adam's expression change and interrupted his thoughts.

"I'm sorry...I did not mean to pry. It's just that it would help to talk to someone who would understand." She reached out to touch his hand.

"It's ok" Adam replied trying to look contrite, carefully concealing his arousal at her touch. "To answer you question" he began as he entwined his fingers with hers, "it was very difficult, but in time it becomes easier. Having someone around also helps and I would like to be that someone for you." Adam gently squeezed her hand in reassurance. Melissa was overcome with emotion, she had never realised that Adam could be this sympathetic and understanding. Smiling at Adam warmly she squeezed his hand in return. Leaning across the table, she gave Adam a quick kiss on the cheek.

"Thank you... " she said.

"No need for thanks, just remember I'm here for you...always. Anyway, let us not dwell on the past. We should be talking about the future. Have you made any decisions about your inheritance?" after a pause he realised he might be rushing her a little. "Forgive me, it's none of my business," he added.

"Funnily enough Suzy asked the same question." It was only then that Melissa realised that Suzy was not at the table and thought that she must have gone to the ladies room. Not giving it any more thought she waited until the waiter, who had returned with their meals, had finished placing them on the table before she carried on.

"I'll have to visit the other estates, to make sure everything is ok. I might even decide to sell them and just keep Fairwinds."

Adam sat in stunned silence. He thought that she had only inherited Fairwinds. He had no idea that there were two other estates. He wanted to laugh aloud. It was too good to be true. He must think of a way to get rid of Suzy, Melissa must only be dependant on him. As he began to eat with gusto, Melissa looked about the restaurant to see if she could spot Suzy. Not seeing any sign of her she decided to give it a few more minutes before she went to check the ladies room and started to eat her own meal.

Suzy wiped her mouth with a tissue and then splashed cold water over her face. She knew she had been in the ladies room for at least fifteen minutes and wondered how long it would be before Melissa came to check. Looking at her pale face in the mirror, she summoned her strength and prepared herself to face him again. Not in the least bit hungry, she did not know if Melissa would guess that something was the matter if she did not eat. The last thing Suzy wanted was for Melissa to worry about her when it was her job to look after Melissa.

Leaving the ladies room she watched Adam and Melissa holding hands across the table as she approached. Trying not to look alarmed, she sat down and was about to say something about her food now being cold, giving her an excuse not to eat. Then she noticed the way Adam was looking at Melissa. Just as she opened her mouth, she closed it shut again as Melissa, barely registering Suzy's return, carried on talking to Adam.

"Although I'm not sure yet, until I go and see them for myself I'm just toying with the idea. I might even decide to sell Fairwinds and live at one of the others. It was actually Suzy's suggestion to go and visit them. Treat it as a holiday." Only then did Melissa look directly at Suzy and smile.

Adam did not like the idea of Melissa traipsing off somewhere without him knowing where she was and he certainly did not like the idea of Suzy being there with her. As he was about to suggest that he could go with her Suzy interrupted.

"That is settled then Melissa, we can start packing tomorrow and leave straight away" Suzy said matter of fact and without looking in Adam's direction. Looking down at her plate, she picked up her fork and moved the food around her plate.

Adam shot a dark look at Suzy and then, quickly masking it, turned his attention back to Melissa.

"Well, we can't really go tomorrow. I still have to sign some papers, but thinking about it now, there is no reason why we could not go beginning of next week. Would you still want to come Suzy?"

"Of course I'm coming with you. I wouldn't miss it and nothing would stop me either." Suzy replied, this time giving

Adam a dark look, which thankfully both Melissa and Adam missed.

"Oh..." said Melissa, suddenly remembering something she wanted to ask Adam. "I noticed a particular portrait of one of your ancestors. Well at least I think it is one of your ancestors. It was the name underneath the picture Adam...it said MacDonnell? Thinking about my estate in Scotland reminded me about it."

Adam ran through the portraits in his mind until he pictured the one he thought Melissa must mean.

"The one of Laird MacDonnell..? Painted in the early Seventeenth century?" He asked in reply. Suzy, suddenly interested in what Adam had to say put her fork down slowly and felt her pulse begin to quicken.

"Yes, that is the one." Melissa answered.

"Let's see." Adam thought back to what his parents had told him about the Laird MacDonnell. "From what I can remember being told he was quite an unsavoury character." Why was that not a surprise Suzy thought privately,

"Really..." Melissa gasped and was immediately intrigued. "Why was he unsavoury?"

"It was said that he raped and pillaged neighbouring clans. Gambled away most of the lands he possessed and was then killed no doubt, in some clan feud as they call them. Apparently, the few remaining clan members scattered having lost their own properties and nearly all but disappeared. Sometime after a recent ancestor, who had emigrated to Canada I believe, amassed a small fortune and returned to England under the name Donell to stop any connections being made. The portrait was one of the few possessions he brought back with him. It was said that the clan MacDonnell is still going strong in Canada. But I have never met any of them."

Suzy gripped her fork tightly as Adam began to tell Melissa about the portrait. Without excusing herself this time, she hurriedly left the table and headed back to the ladies room. Melissa, fascinated by what Adam was saying, did not pay any attention to Suzy's abrupt departure. When

Suzy reached the toilet, she vomited once more and splashed her face afterwards in cold water. Could that be the connection she wondered, Suzy mulled it over in her mind. Could it be that simple? She knew she had to act fast and get Melissa away from Adam as soon as possible. She did not like the way he looked at her and she could not believe that Melissa was even contemplating Adam in any intimate way. No doubt it had crossed her mind, as Suzy hadn't missed some of the looks Melissa had graced Adam with. Rinsing her mouth out, she looked at her watch. She had been gone another fifteen minutes and really did not want to face Adam right now. How he could so casually mention the words rape and pillage in front of her without even a wince made Suzy angry and determined that he would never be able to do the same thing to anyone else. The sudden thought of telling Melissa, came and went swiftly... she just needed more time and some more answers that seemed tantalising beyond her. Perhaps she would just have to gain the courage to do so before it was too late. Shuddering, Suzy left the sanctuary of the ladies room and paused at the door to glance over to where they were sitting. Oh my god she thought...Adam has just lent over to kiss Melissa...what could have transpired in such a short time? Suzy practically rushed the rest of the way back to the table. As she reached them she just caught the last thing Melissa said to Adam.

"Adam you have been wonderful company this evening. You have made me laugh and the history regarding your ancestors was absolutely fascinating. Thank you. I would really like to do this again and soon."

"Most definitely, perhaps I could ring you in a couple of days. Or is that too soon?"

"No that would be fine...I look forward to it." Melissa stood up and then looked at Suzy, "ah there you are. I think that maybe I have had a little too much wine. I was just about to call a taxi to go home."

Relief washed over Suzy. At last... she thought they were leaving. Adam, still going over the possible value of

Melissa's estates in his mind could not believe it was going to be easier than he first thought. Melissa, feeling relaxed and even a little aroused was genuinely looking forward to seeing Adam again in a couple of days.

The waiter appeared once more with the bill. Adam reached out and told Melissa he would take care of it.

"Thanks again Adam. I'll see you soon." Melissa then led the way out of the restaurant and into the lobby, where she fumbled for her mobile and rang for a taxi. Suzy had followed behind closely, thoughts whirling around in her mind about Melissa, Adam and that dammed portrait.

Adam sat at the table waiting for the waiter to bring him his change, with a smugly sinister smile on his lips.

CHAPTER ELEVEN

Melissa awoke the following morning feeling happier than she had for the past few weeks and was contemplating the day ahead when thoughts of Adam kept popping into her mind. Smiling to herself, she recalled the gentleness in his eyes as he looked at her and the fluttering she felt when he leaned over to kiss her lightly. Glancing across to the huge window, she spotted the sun peeking through the gap in the heavy curtains. Getting out of bed she walked over to the window and pulled them back, letting the warmth of the sun bathe her face. Sighing to herself she turned and made her way to the bathroom to shower and wash. As the water refreshed her, she realised that this was the first morning that she hadn't been filled with sadness at waking up in her parent's house now that they were gone. Stepping out from the shower and walking back into her bedroom she was drawn to the pendant that lay next to her bed. It sparkled brilliantly in the sunlight and while looking at the beautiful array of every shade of green she could imagine, she decided that today she should go to the solicitor's office and get the paperwork out of the way. The pendant seemed to sparkle even brighter in reply.

Suzy awoke in a very different mood. She had tossed and turned all night and had very little sleep. She did not understand what had caused the change in Melissa. Why was it now that she was thinking of Adam in a different light? ...Adam...after all this time, still trying to impress Melissa and putting on a complete act. Of that, Suzy was sure. Why though...? Suzy did not know. Something was not right. Just what was it that she had to do? The sooner we go to Scotland the better...hopefully Melissa might be distracted enough to forget about Adam. Just being with him made her think about what he had done to her and even though she still felt ashamed, she felt angry. Suzy decided that was a good thing and that maybe her anger would help her face up to him. Feeling slightly better she got out of bed and without bothering to get dressed, wrapped herself in her gown and went down to the kitchen to make some breakfast.

When she reached the kitchen, she saw Melissa already sitting down, eating some toast. Melissa smiled and said good morning to Suzy, pointing to the toaster.

"There are a couple slices left, if you want them."

"Thanks" Suzy replied and went to help herself. Joining Melissa at the table she noticed that Melissa was humming a tune while munching on her toast.

"You seem happier this morning," she remarked.

"Hmmm, yes I do." Melissa replied in between a bite of toast and a sip of coffee. "I have even decided to make an appointment with Mr Mackenzie and sign all the paperwork. Hopefully he can fit me in sometime today." Suzy brightened at the mention of Melissa's solicitor.

"That is good. Have you phoned already or would you like me to go and get your mobile? There's no time like the present, so they say." Melissa laughed at Suzy's eagerness.

"No I haven't phoned yet. It's only just gone 9 o'clock..." Watching Suzy fold her arms and sit back, Melissa relented. "Oh, go on then, my phone's still in my bag. It should still be on the side table in the entrance hall." Suzy got up and practically ran out of the kitchen to fetch Melissa's bag. Returning, she passed the phone over to Melissa and sat down again. Melissa scrolled through her phonebook until she found the number for 'Mackenzie and Sons' and pressed dial.

"Good morning, you are through to the office of Conrad Mackenzie. How may I help?"

"Yes, good morning. It's Melissa Conway, I was wondering if it's at all possible to rearrange the appointment

I had to cancel a few day's ago." For some reason Melissa began to feel nervous.

"Of course, let me have a look at the diary. When would it be convenient for you?"

"Um...would today be ok?"

"Ah, I'm afraid Mr Mackenzie won't be in today. I could make the appointment for tomorrow?"

"Oh...I was rather hoping to get it all over and done with today, but I guess tomorrow will be fine." Melissa sounded a little disappointed.

"Shall I put you down for 10 o'clock Miss Conway? Or would you like a later appointment as there is space in the afternoon?"

"No, that is fine, I mean 10 o'clock would be fine, thank you."

"Thank you Miss Conway. Can I help you with anything else?"

"No, that was all, thank you again." Melissa said goodbye and hung up.

Mrs Collins, Conrad's secretary, placed the receiver back on the cradle. She had not been entirely honest with Miss Conway and felt a little guilty. Conrad had in fact not been to the office for the past two day's and she did not even know if he would make an appearance tomorrow. Perhaps she should give him a call, just to see if he was any better. After all he might be interested to know that Miss Conway had rescheduled her appointment. She had not missed the look on his face when Miss Conway had cancelled her previous one and also had not missed the way he sat in his office that day poring over Miss Conway's file again and again before going home. Picking up the phone she decided to give him a call straight away.

"Hello Mr Mackenzie, how are you feeling today?" Mrs Collins asked in her usual businesslike tone.

"I'm fine Mrs Collins, feeling much better thank you. Perhaps you were right. I have probably been overdoing it at work recently. A couple of days off have done me the world of good. I was actually going to ring you later, I'll be back in the office tomorrow."

Mrs Collins thought that Conrad did indeed sound much better and considered not telling him that Miss Conway had phoned and instead wait until he came in tomorrow morning. However, she had never been one to stand in the way of two people. For a moment she considered Conrad's recent behaviour and her experience told her that perhaps there was a little more to it than what met the eye.

"Oh...Mr Mackenzie, this could probably wait, but I received a call from Miss Conway. She has rescheduled her appointment for tomorrow. Actually she did ask to come in today, but with you not being here I put her in for 10 o'clock tomorrow." At the mention of Melissa, Conrad's mood heightened even more.

"Thanks Mrs Collins," he paused before continuing. "Actually I could come in this afternoon. Could you phone Miss Conway back and tell her that if she still wants to come to the offices today that I will be in. Shall we say about 2pm?"

"Yes of course Mr Mackenzie." Mrs Collin's sat with a knowing smile on her lips and after pressing for a new line she rang Miss Conway's number.

Melissa was out in the garden reading when Mrs Collins rang back and was delighted to hear she could finalise everything that day. Suzy was also looking forward to it, but for different reasons entirely!

As they approached the offices they both looked up as a long, sleek, black saloon car with tinted windows pulled up just outside the office. A rather tall, fat, middle aged, bald headed man stepped from the car. He looked at the two girls who watched him from the pavement, both openly curious. One girl in particular caught his eye and he seemed to squint as he tried to focus on her face. Melissa and Suzy saw the man staring intently and involuntary stepped back. He appeared not to notice and carried on staring. As though something seemed to register, he smiled coldly and then walked up the steps to the entrance. Without waiting, he pushed through the doors and went in.

"He was kinda creepy. Did you see the way he looked at us?" Suzy remarked to Melissa.

"Oh, it was probably nothing. Most middle-aged, bald men look like that when they see one gorgeous female, let alone two." Melissa said, matter of fact, and broke out into a huge grin. Suzy, grinning in reply, told Melissa she was probably right. They reached the entrance and Melissa looked at the brass plaque to make sure they had the right building.

"Does not look much like a solicitor's office," Suzy said while looking at the elegant facade. "I mean it still looks like a lived in townhouse, right out of Oliver Twist!" Smiling at Suzy, Melissa had to agree. It certainly was not what she was expecting. She pressed the buzzer and then pushed open the door. As they stepped into the inner hall they both felt they had indeed stepped back in time. An open fire was burning gently in the hearth, on the walls were oil painted portraits and pictures and to the side of the huge ornamental fireplace were two over stuffed leather sofas that looked as though you would sink as soon as you sat down. All they could do was stare at the opulent surroundings. Looking around they saw alcoves that had been made into bookshelves, an antique lamp, which adorned the rustic coffee table and décor that was rich in colour but appeared subtle. Another door opened just then and Mrs Collins appeared.

"Good Afternoon, you must be Miss Conway," and she held out her hand. Melissa shook it firmly and then followed Mrs Collins through the door from where she had appeared, leaving Suzy still open mouthed, staring around the room as though in a film set. She was led into a second waiting area, which Melissa assumed to be an outer office, as in one corner there was a desk and chair, filing cabinets and a copier machine. There was a door, which was marked private and a second door with Mr Mackenzie etched into the glass. She was unable to see through, as there was some sort of blind pulled down giving privacy to those inside.

"Please take a seat and I'll let Mr Mackenzie know you are here." Mrs Collins pointed to another overstuffed leather sofa, but still looking about her Melissa noticed that this room was in complete contrast to the entrance hall. Contemporary décor graced the walls with only two abstract prints for decoration. Again there were bookshelves, but these were modern with a mixture of travel and reference books instead of the thick heavy looking tomes in the entrance. It was light and airy with decorative plants placed haphazardly. As she sat and waited, a slight fluttering in her stomach began but she did not know why she was feeling nervous. Touching her pendant, she felt calmer and relaxed a little. She wondered briefly if the man they had seen outside was in the office now and that is why she was waiting. Maybe the secretary who had entered his office had interrupted them. Looking at her watch she noticed it had only been a few minutes but it felt longer. Crossing her legs, then uncrossing them, she glanced around again twiddling her fingers. Mrs Collins reappeared and held the door leading to Mr Mackenzie's office open for Melissa to go in. Hmmm...maybe that man worked here she thought.

As she walked into Conrad's office she expected him to be waiting for her, but instead he was nowhere to be seen. She noticed that his office also had two doors leading off from it and wondered where they led too; before her curiosity got the better of her, she sat down quickly. The nervousness returned tenfold and she began to feel queasy. Straightening her back in an effort to look calm and composed, a picture hanging on the wall caught her interest and for a moment, her queasiness abated.

It was the most beautiful painting she had ever seen. The landscape in the painting seemed to come alive with the colours that had been used. It reminded her of all the daydreams she had when she was young. A castle stood majestically to one side of the picture with snow-capped mountains in the background. A river of some sort appeared from between the mountains and weaved its way over the canvas towards the viewer. The sky was interlaced with blues, pinks and purples, as though depicting a subset in a far off magical land, a low stone bridge spanned the water that could be seen linking the castle with the land on the other side. Amidst a vividly green pasture, dotted with bright wildflowers, there stood a single willow tree, its branches gently teasing the waters surface. Underneath there was a woman seated on a white horse with her long dark hair blowing behind her, while a man stood at the horse's side. Melissa imagined they were lovers as her head was inclined towards the man, as though listening to what he was saying, while his hand rested on her thigh. Lost in the painting, Melissa felt a pang of longing and regret she did not understand. She really did have a fanciful imagination...she thought.

Conrad entered his office silently and stood just inside the door studying Melissa as she stared at the painting intently. She did not even turn around when he clicked the door softly shut. He wondered what she was thinking about staring at the picture like that. Just then he swore he heard a voice come from somewhere deep inside. Loath to interrupt her oneness with the painting he began to feel a powerful urge to go over and touch her. Trying to control the urging he stood there for a few moments more then found himself walking over to her. Coughing habitually, he announced his presence.

Startled, Melissa turned around and looked up in surprise at Conrad standing a mere breath away. Not knowing whether to stay seated or stand, she folded her hands in her lap. Sensing her hesitation went briskly around to his side of the desk and sat down forgoing a formal greeting. He paused for a moment and without looking directly at her began to speak at the same time Melissa did.

"Thank you for seeing me..."

"Thank you for coming..."

Both sat staring at each other until Conrad could not help an enormous grin from spreading across his face. Just then, Melissa was reminded of someone but she shook her head clear.

"I'm sorry...you first," Conrad said still grinning.

"Oh...yes...sorry, I just wanted to thank you for seeing me on such short notice." Melissa briefly thought of Suzy waiting outside and made a note to tell her that maybe she was right. Melissa had to admit his grin made him devastatingly handsome. Adam popped into her mind just then and feeling a little guilty she rushed on.

"Will it take long to sign the paperwork?" she asked. Taken aback slightly by her sudden abruptness Conrad automatically reached for the documents laid out on his desk.

"Err... no, not at all" all traces of his grin now gone. Glancing at the painting Melissa had studied, he still wanted to ask her what she was thinking about when she looked at it when he thought he heard another voice in his mind urging him on again. Melissa spoke interrupting his thoughts.

"Would you like me to just sign at the bottom of each one?" She asked holding a pen ready.

"You should really read through them before you sign but yes, at the bottom of each one will be fine." Conrad did not understand her sudden change and would never normally let one of his client's just sign a document without reading it, but he sensed that she was uncomfortable for some reason and was in a rush to leave.

"Please don't think I'm being rude but wouldn't you like to go through the details pertaining to your estates?" Conrad actually sounded surprised at himself for asking her and briefly forgot about the voice urging him on. Melissa looked up from the document she had signed and regarded Conrad for an instant. She had to get out of here as quickly as possible. She almost could not breath, she felt light headed, as though she was about to faint and she had no idea as to why when she felt perfectly fine this morning. She had not meant to sound abrupt earlier either, but she could not help it. It was almost as though it was someone else speaking instead of her. The room seemed smaller too and the air thicker, colder. Touching her pendant, she hoped it would give her some comfort and make her feel at ease as it normally did. Instead it was hot... almost too hot to touch... so she let go and again answered him abruptly,

"No need, thank you...I'll be visiting them shortly so I'll find out what I need to know then." Melissa visibly blushed. Conrad did not miss it and was more confused and intrigued than ever. He watched her as she touched the pendant and his eyes opened wider as he imagined the pendant glowing. Blinking once more, he was convinced he must be seeing things and perhaps he should have taken some more time off work. He then wondered why she snatched her hand away as if burnt. Shaking his head mentally, he had never felt so off balance before. The voice in his head was now persistent and almost shouting this time, but still he made no sense of it. Trying to push everything from his mind he got up and stared out of the window behind his desk. Melissa wanted the ground to open up and swallow her. Never had she been so rude to anyone.

All of a sudden she laughed. Conrad spun around. He had had just about enough. She might be the most striking woman he had ever laid eyes on and he was sure that somehow his mind had put her in several of his dreams in different guises, but he was not going to stand there and be laughed at for no reason. It was all beyond him. Melissa, head bent, felt outrageous and ashamed, but was filled with a mischief she could not explain. Hurrying her last signature, she passed all the documents across the desk and got up.

"All done..." As much as she wanted to apologise the words would not form on her lips. Conrad grunted a reply and looked right past her, his mind battered and baffled. Melissa left the office quickly. Never had she behaved so inexcusably. As the door closed behind her Conrad looked across to the painting and from nowhere he breathed the name...Maura...

CHAPTER TWELVE

Melissa made her way back to her car still blushing furiously, she simply could not fathom why she had behaved the way she had. Suzy greeted her in the waiting room with a thousand and one questions, but Melissa in a hurry to leave the building just told her they had to go straight away. Once she reached her car she looked across to Suzy and apologised, who by this time had given up and could also not understand why Melissa had left in such a rush.

"I'm sorry Suzy for practically running out of there. I..." she could not even begin to explain. Suzy was dumbstruck, as Melissa never in all the time she had known her appeared so flustered.

"What happened in his office?" She asked thinking it must have been something really awful.

"Oh Suzy, it was dreadful. I mean... I was absolutely dreadful!" Suzy's eyes widened, in a mixture of mirth and amazement at Melissa's admission.

"You...! You are never dreadful." Although dying to hear what had happened, but remembering they still had not got into the car she opened her door with a flourish. As she got in she told Melissa to get in the car too and tell her about it on the way home. Melissa did as she was told, still shocked. Only starting to relax a little the more distance she put between herself and Mr Mackenzie's office and managed to navigate the busier parts of London with ease. When they got out on to the motorway, Suzy continued where she left off.

"What exactly did you mean by dreadful? As I'm sure it was not as bad as you think."

"Oh, but Suzy, it was. As soon as I entered his office I became nervous and fidgety, which as you know, is completely unlike me."

"Yes, but that is understandable, given the circumstances."

"No, no it was different."

"Different?" Now Suzy was definitely dying to know what happened. "Go on..."

"Well, while I was waiting in the outer room to his office I noticed it was completely different to the one in which you were waiting..."

"So... That is irrelevant...you are killing me here!" Suzy chuckled, while looking completely innocent at Melissa.

"Humph..." Melissa grunted good-naturedly. "That is when it started...the nervousness. Then I was led in to his actual office." Even the seat belt Suzy wore could not stop her from leaning closer as Melissa began to explain. "He was not even in there and I began to feel more nervous."

Suzy just rolled her eyes and sat back. "There were two doors that led from his office, one I think must of led to a bathroom and another...I don't know where that led to. But I started to feel sick too as well as nervous." She looked across to Suzy and sighed.

"That is only natural though Mel, I thought you had done something awful, but it sounds all perfectly reasonable to me."

"I know, but there was this painting. It was the most beautiful painting I have ever seen and it reminded me about the daydreams I used to have as a child." Suzy caught the look of wistfulness on Melissa's face and her interest returned.

"What was the picture of?"

"I can only assume it was somewhere in Scotland, there was snow capped mountains, a castle, a loch or perhaps a river and two people, a man and a woman. The woman was seated on a magnificent horse and it looked as though she was bending down to hear whatever the man was saying to her. I no longer felt nervous or sick but I felt a deep sense of loss, I can't explain it, after all it was just a painting." Melissa sighed deeply.

Suzy knew that Melissa was a pure romantic, she herself had listened to Melissa reminisce about her childhood fantasies when the were at school together, but she was a little concerned that a painting would have such an effect on a grown woman and put it down the recent loss of her mother. Perhaps Melissa would look at anything now in a different way.

"That still does not explain why you thought you acted dreadfully." Suzy remarked.

"It was, I think a mixture of different things, first the nervousness and the feeling sick, then the painting, the reason I was there. When Mr Mackenzie eventually appeared in his office I was momentarily taken in by his smile. It was warm, friendly and made him look devastatingly delicious. It gave me delightful little shivers and we both began to speak at the same time. He simply grinned at me and it reminded me of someone, you know like deja vu." Suzy's eyes were even wider and after all she would have to agree entirely, she thought he was a dish anyway. But for Melissa to remark on how it made her feel was especially surprising to say the least.

"When he grinned at me that way, it felt so familiar. Then I immediately thought of Adam and felt guilty I suppose."

"Guilty! What an earth for?" Suzy blurted. "Adam is nothing." Melissa missed the note of disgust in Suzy's last sentence.

"I like Adam and it is wrong to get all excited over another man, especially over a simple smile. Along with everything else I was feeling, I acted rudely towards Mr Mackenzie. I rushed through all the paperwork signing it without even reading it and to top it all off, when I knew Mr Mackenzie was not entirely impressed with my behaviour, I felt his annoyance and simply burst out laughing! I was unable to help myself Suzy, so I rushed out without even saying goodbye!"

Suzy was completely speechless and understood why Melissa had thought she'd behaved dreadfully. It was totally against her character to do anything remotely like what she had done earlier. Usually so calm and composed, especially given the circumstances would normally have been reservedly proper and demure. The rest of the journey home was made in silence each turning over the events of the morning in their minds.

They reached Fairwinds and still silent, got out of the car. It was not until they entered that Melissa spoke again.

"I was planning on asking Adam if he would like to meet for lunch today. Do you want to join us?"

Suzy immediately made an excuse not to go and although she wanted Melissa to talk some more about how she felt. Knew by the change of subject that she was not going to offer anymore information. Making her way up to her room she left Melissa downstairs humming to herself.

Hmmm...Suzy thought I have to get her away from Adam as soon as I can. Perhaps I could suggest going to Scotland now that the paperwork had been signed. Dinner now lunch...she had a hunch that Adam was up to something and did not like it one bit.

Melissa pushing the events of the morning out of her mind phoned Adam to make arrangements for lunch. She was actually looking forward to seeing him again. Mrs Betts answered after three rings.

"Afternoon Mrs Betts is Adam available, its Melissa."

"Why yes Miss Conway. I'll go and get him for you straight away." Melissa only had to wait a few moments before she heard Adams voice down the line.

"Melissa, Its good to hear from you so soon. To what do I owe the pleasure?" Hearing his smooth deep voice made her feel warm inside and thoughts of Conrad vanished as she stood holding the receiver smiling into it.

"I just thought I'd phone and see if you were free for lunch today. Don't worry if you can't, I know its a bit short notice and its not really lunchtime anymore, but I thought it would be rather nice."

"It would be absolutely wonderful. Tell you what, why don't I come and pick you up and we'll decide where to go when I get there? Say in about thirty minutes?"

"Yes. That would be great. See you in thirty minutes then. Bye for now."

"Goodbye Melissa."

Adam could not believe his luck. As he replaced the receiver, a plan started to take shape in his mind. After a few minutes, he left the study intent on what he needed to do. Mrs Betts passed him on her way upstairs with some laundry. She was just about to ask about Melissa, when she noticed the look on his face and very nearly dropped the bundle she was carrying. It was eerily unnatural. Hurriedly she continued on her way muttering under her breath. Even after all these years, she still remained slightly wary of him. Shivering slightly, she thought back to the time he had lost both his parents in that terrible accident. She had come across him then, just as she had now and shivered again as she remembered seeing the same look on his face. Unable to explain why it frightened her a little, she simply clucked her tongue. Reaching the large cupboard on the upper landing, she put the clean bedding away and put it to the back of her mind.

Oblivious to Mrs Betts, Adam raced up the stairs and passed her on the way as he made his way to his room. With a quick change of shirt and a glance in the mirror, he was ready. Feeling confidant and in control he strolled casually back down the stairs and left the house without a backward glance. He arrived at Fairwinds in a matter of minutes and was surprised and pleased that Melissa was already waiting on the steps outside. Stopping directly in front of her he jumped out and ran around the car to open the door for her. As she brushed past him he inhaled her perfume and felt immediately aroused by the scent. It lingered in his nostrils as he made his way back around the car and he got back in hoping she would not notice. After greeting one another, Adam suggested they try out a new bistro, which he had recently seen advertised. Melissa agreed and so they continued on their way making pleasant small talk.

Suzy looking out from an upstairs window frowned as she watched Melissa getting into Adams car. Determined to take matters into her own hands, she pulled her suitcase down from the top of the wardrobe and dragged it across the floor hoisting it onto the bed. Grabbing all her clothes from inside the wardrobe, she carelessly threw them in the case and sat on top of it. As soon as Melissa returns, we have to get away from here...

CHAPTER THIRTEEN

'Maura? I do not know anyone called Maura. Who the hell was Maura?" Conrad was still standing in the middle of his office after Melissa's abrupt departure, over thirty minutes ago and repeated the name several more times, thoroughly confused. He began pacing back and forth in his office when Mrs Collins knocked at the door and stepped in.

"I hope I'm not interrupting." She said as he continued to pace. Glancing at his secretary from the corner of his eye he stopped and turned to face her.

"No... not at all Mrs Collins." She was doubtful of his reply but stepped further into the office. She placed the parcel, which had mysteriously disappeared a few days ago and had reappeared on her desk just as mysteriously only moments ago, on his desk. Without taking her eyes of it, she took a step back.

"Ah I see. The post... thank you." Walking back to his desk from the opposite side of his office, where she had found him, he stood next to Mrs Collins and picked up the small box that she had put down. He turned it over in his hand and felt the hairs on the back of his neck rise. He put it down hastily.

"No... not this morning's post Mr Mackenzie, it is the parcel that went missing. I came back and found it sitting on my desk."

Immediately Conrad's senses were alerted and questioning. He looked quizzically at Mrs Collins, waiting for an explanation. Noticing the look of uncertainty on his face, emphasised by his eyebrow raised in suspicion, she continued hesitantly.

"After Miss Conway left in such a hurry, I debated with myself whether or not to ask you if there had been a problem. I must say I was surprised by her abrupt departure as much as I was at you remaining in your office for twenty minutes without summoning me afterwards. When I finally made my mind up, I thought it would be a good idea to bring you some coffee and find out what happened. I know that perhaps you might think it uncharacteristic, but I felt that, out of concern, you understand. I simply felt it was necessary. You have been somewhat out of sorts of late..." Conrad interrupted before she could finish and she faced him squarely, closing her mouth firmly shut.

"Yes, well, thank you for your concern, but that still does not explain how you found the parcel to be sitting on your desk, as you say. Someone must have left it there."

"I thought so too, until I looked at the records. No one has been here today except Miss Conway. I went to get you a coffee and when I returned, there it was" She swallowed audibly, still unsure herself where it could have come from and took a further step back.

"That is impossible!" Someone must have left it. Things, especially parcels don't just disappear then reappear when they want." In the space it took for him to take his next breath he heard a quiet voice whisper...can't they?

"What did you just say?" He straightened to his full height and leaned over Mrs Collins.

"I did not say anything Mr Mackenzie." A little stunned at his sharp accusation, she too stiffened her spine and raised her chin. Relaxing only slightly, he stepped back from Mrs Collins as he sensed she was telling the truth. Of that he had no doubt. He had been hearing voices much to often lately for his liking and nothing seemed to be making much sense these days. An uneasy calm settled around him and slowly he turned away from Mrs Collins.

"Perhaps they came when you weren't there and they could not wait."

"Perhaps" she replied to appease him and left the office. She knew assuredly that no one could have been to the office in her absence as she had locked the door. Which in her mind, begged the question, just how did it find its way to her desk?

After his secretary left, he walked slowly around his desk, staring at the parcel intently. He half expected something to jump out from the small box and silently cursed himself for being foolish.

Admittedly he was intrigued to know what was inside so he sat down and lowered his head to take a closer look at it, before picking it up. His usually perceptive intuition told him nothing and this time he felt no shivers at the back of his neck, so he relaxed a little. On closer examination, he noticed that the label had been written on in very old fashioned handwriting, which although not exactly odd, was not commonly seen in today's ready printed labels. He shook the box lightly and heard a soft rustle from inside. Hmmm... probably contained nothing important, Oh well... it can probably wait until I get home.

Normally any personal mail that required immediate attention stated so on the label. But the label on this parcel was simply addressed to a...

Mr Conrad Mackenzie, confidential, to be opened by addressee only...

Placing the box gently back on his desk he sat for a few moments going over the meeting he had earlier with Miss Conway. She certainly was not what he expected her to be like and decided that maybe he should just forget all about her. Picking up his case, he went over to collect his jacket from the shiny chrome stand that complemented the rest of the sparse furnishings and buzzed through to Mrs Collins to let her know he was going out and probably would not return to the office that day. Then he picked up the small box and put it into his briefcase. An almighty rumble from deep within his stomach pushed all his other thoughts away. Leaving only one... food.

Letting himself in to his apartment he hung up his jacket and carried his briefcase into the kitchen with him. His stomach becoming louder the nearer he got to the kitchen. Leaving at the doorway he opened the fridge and grabbed some of the previous nights pizza. He made himself a drink then balancing a plate on top of the cup he precariously bent to retrieve his case on the way out and walked into the lounge trying not to drop anything. Making his way safely and without incident he slowly lowered the cup onto the table and sunk into his oversized leather sofa, swinging his case up to land beside him. Fumbling for the remote control between the cushions he eventually found it and switched on the TV from where he was sitting. Biting into the pizza his stomach made one more growl in anticipation then eventually stopped as he finished the pizza. Flicking idly through the hundreds of channels he could not find anything of interest, Unbelievable... Not one blasted thing on and fleeting thought about cancelling his subscription. Only changing his mind when he came across a documentary about Garry Kasparov who is considered one of the greatest chess players of all time. Even though Conrad did not play chess as much as he would like to, his instinctive and intuitive mind understood the game and all its intricacies more than most. Winning easily came naturally to him, in the few local tournaments he had entered in recent years. Making himself more comfortable on the sofa he nudged his case and remembered the parcel. Opening his briefcase, he took the parcel out to see what it contained.

Examining it closely he noticed there was no postmark. Strange...he murmured. It could not possibly have been delivered by hand... Turning it over gently as it appeared to be quite old, he unwrapped the outer packaging carefully, feeling its slightly stiff yet yellowing age with his fingers. It appeared to be wrapped in a type of old parchment. That is unusual... he thought... Putting the wrapping to one side he turned the box over once more in his hands. It was simply a plain wooden box made out of oak with no visible markings; there were no etchings or writing either to give away its contents, or from where and who it had come. He located a tiny, worn and slightly rusty catch, which at first he found to be a bit fiddly, due to his large hands and thick fingers. Concentrating all his efforts on working it loose he nearly jumped when he heard the loud snap as the lid fell open. As it fell open his eyes widen in disbelief. All it contained was a single white envelope, no bigger than a postcard. He reached inside to dislodge the envelope from the box. The barest touch of his fingertips on the envelope as he retrieved it sent shock waves through his body causing him to jolt unexpectedly. As though struck by an unseen force, powerful and insistent he felt trapped in the midst of a fierce storm from where there was no escape. He had no control. Anger, pain and suffering culminated into a torrent of emotions that rampaged mercilessly through his body. Never had he feared anything before now. Gripping the nearest thing to hand, he snapped the remote control in two, so great was the unknown force possessing him. His Rage could not overcome it. Throwing himself back into the sofa did little to stop the madness. He tried to fight it he lashed out randomly but to no avail. It was much more powerful than he. Something greater than he ever thought existed was taking over, pushing away his soul and replacing it with another. Random images rushed at him of people's faces that he did not know and places of great beauty flashed before his very eyes. Hushed voices, chanting in unison were becoming louder and louder. He felt lost in a place he neither knew nor could ever have imagined. His mind was crazy and fearful, his whole body became rigidly taut and his skin glistened with sweat. With a strength born out of fear, he stood up only to fall to his knees and he gripped his pounding head, trying to block out the noise. A sound, similar to a lone wolf howling its pain and anguish at being separated from its pack, carried through the air as though from a distance. Dimly he realised it was his own voice. Closing his eyes in a weak attempt to wipe out the images he caught the briefest glimpse of the envelope as it fell from his fingers.

As it floated to the ground majestically and knowingly, everything around him came to an abrupt stop. Afraid to move, he waited until his breathing steadied and his heart stopped hammering wildly. Very slowly, he began to relax and he looked down at the floor where the envelope now lay with a mixture of dread and fascination. He felt different. He was now different. Sitting back on his haunches, he wiped the sweat away from his brow. The room was still and silent except for the steady rhythm of his heart. Fear had now been replaced by an unnatural calm and he filled his lungs with a huge gulp of air, as though tasting it for the first time. His fingers went automatically to the envelope and when he picked it up this time he gripped it tightly. Now you will understand...an inner voice said clearer than ever before. He no longer was afraid of the voice he heard. He knew now that it was part of him and he felt at peace.

He opened the envelope slowly and took out what looked like a letter. Gently he unfolded it and began to read.

If ye are reading this then ye must be Conrad Mackenzie who was born on the 11th June in the year 1974. I am na letter writer and believe me when I say that Brietta is a sly auld one, I be na knowing at the time if what she told me would come to pass. So forgive me if this makes no sense to you as it made na sense to me when she told mi.

I will try tae explain as best I can. It disna seem possible even as I write this tae ye, that in its self some would say is madness and I still shake mi head in fear and in hope. Ye see mi love for Maura...och, let me tell ye about Maura. She was the bonniest lass in all the Highlands and I know now that I loved her from the first time I set eyes on her. She was but a wee lass and I not much aulder. She looked at mi with those huge, round, green eyes, unlike no other shade I hae seen afore or since. Her eyes...they fascinated mi, hunted mi and had depths that could bring not just mi, ye understand, but any man to his knees. How I miss her.

We shared what precious moments we could, sometimes down by the burn, other times under our favourite Oak tree, but never for more than a few hours and always in secret. Except the last time I saw her. It was also the only time we had spent more than just a few hours together. It was the most...well anyways, its now't ye need know about. The next morn I went tae dae battle wi the MacDonnell's, a bloody battle it was too. I was injured and left tae rot, there on the ground. A group of traveller's, gypsies they be, for some reason I still canna fathom. Picked mi up and took me wi them. All I know is that I must hae been gone for several moons. For I regained mi strength and an overgrown beard to go wi it and healed wi no visible scar. I ne'er questioned how or why, some things are better left well alone. When I eventually returned to my clan, there was much celebration and even suspicion. It was nearly a sennicht afore I tried to contact Maura. When I did,

I cudna find her. That was when Brietta sent mi a message asking to meet her.

She told mi of Maura...tis tae painful tae speak of, even now. She then foretold of a boy, who would be born on the same day as ye and given your name, He would be a direct descendant of mine. He would be the first son to be born whose soul would leave him at his first breath. I'm sorry lad tae hae to be the one tae tell ye that if ye didna know, but that is the way of things. It wud be mi own soul that wud breath life back into ye and allow mi tae be wi her again.

I ken wha ye must be thinking, I thought it tae, but ye see Brietta made sure things wud come tae pass, as they should. If she'd be right then I think ye ken I'm right. She also said that ye might fight it, as it wud cause ye pain and fear. I believe there'd be a reason as tae why I'd hae to wait for two hundred years and several generations and that be caus she wud be here in yer time. Tis now up to ye. Find her afore its tae late...

Conrad read and reread the letter several times torn between astonishment and disbelief he tried to remain objective and logical. Certainly he felt different, but was that why? A thousand questions collided inside his head. Who would have the answers? Would there be anyone alive who was able to answer? He wondered if that is why he had been feeling strange of late. Was it more than just working too much? Was this the real reason things he had felt all those things, heard voices and had those vivid dreams? He did not know. It could not be true. Could it...? If he believed for one minute it was true. It went against all he had been taught and all he had believed in. Things like this just did not happen. It was all nonsense, some sick twisted joke. He would have to check to see if anyone he had put behind bars had been released in recent weeks. That was it.... had to be it...someone was simply seeking revenge. It occurred to him then that there could be no other reason. The alternative of course was simply unthinkable.

He crumpled the letter into a tight ball and threw it effortlessly into the waste paper bin. Slowly he got up and went into the kitchen. His head was beginning to pound again. Reaching into the highest cupboard he took out some painkillers that helped him also to sleep and swallowed two without water. He then poured himself a large whiskey, not heeding the health warning and gulped the contents down in one gulp. Not bothering to switch of the lights or the television he went straight to his bedroom, kicking the door shut behind him. Collapsing onto his bed he soon fell into a deep but restless sleep.

... Maura! Maura!" her mother called in a raspy shout. 'Where could that girl be?' she sat pitifully in her chair, knowing her body was becoming weaker each day and she worried constantly about her daughter's future. Now she was even too weak to refill her cup of water. Where was Maura when she needed her? A slight smile hovered over her lips as she imagined Maura was probably down by the burn daydreaming as usual. She was sometimes thankful that her daughter had such a vivid imagination and delighted in the stories she told as they sat around the fire each evening. It was a gift from god, of that she was certain and thanked him silently.

Looking up at the sky she noticed the clouds were rolling slightly faster and becoming darker. She pulled her threadbare shawl tighter around her shoulders but still felt the bitterness of a crisp wind snake around her bare legs and pierce her skin through the gaps. The threat of a storm was clear. She could almost taste it as she moistened her dry lips. Again she tried to summon her strength to lift the cup to her lips and knew she would also have to take cover inside. Successfully she manoeuvred herself into a better position to be able to lift herself up and reach for the cup when she caught a glimpse of Maura just as she felt the first drops of rain. Stunned momentarily by the person who was with her, she stumbled back into the chair, not noticing the rain becoming heavier. It was obvious from where she sat that Maura had not yet noticed her sitting there as she dashed towards a small corpse of trees, with what looked like a boy or was it a young man? Despite trying to peer closer she could not quite make out who it was. 'Amazing...' She whispered aloud hoarsely, Maura had never mentioned anybody to her and actually felt a little disappointed. Why would she keep it a secret from her, they were so close, or so she thought.

Feeling not only cold but now wet through as well she just about managed to pull herself up slowly and go inside, each small movement making her breathing more difficult. Even after all these years, she still remained surprised at how quickly a storm could descend upon them and then after causing havoc gently abate, leaving the most glorious scent of heather rise up from the ground and a fresh cotton like scent hanging in the air. She glanced back towards Maura and the person she was with before closing the door and watched in awe as the man leaned in closer putting his arms around Maura protecting her from the storm. Realising she had left her cup outside she went over to makeshift cupboard and pulled out another one. As she poured herself another cup of water she wondered about the man with Maura. Maybe she would not have to worry so much about Maura's future after all.

It was true, Maura had not noticed her mother as she and Ciar raced for cover under the trees. He had come across her in her usual place by the burn and had been teasing her when he too had looked up towards the sky and predicted a storm brewing. Maura intent on trying to best him sat stubbornly on the ground refusing to believe him, until she felt a fat blob of rain fall indignantly onto the tip of her nose. Feeling decidedly mortified she got up so quickly Ciar had to reach out to stop her from tripping over her own foot. She could not help but smile reluctantly as Ciar began laughing, unable to keep it in anymore. He stopped for a moment and their eyes met as Maura pushed back a damp lock of hair from her face. Just as she was about to tuck it behind her ear he reached out to stop her and gently removing her hand he held the damp lock of hair with his own. He became fascinated by the silky thickness as he twirled it around his fingers and felt compelled to raise it to his nostril and breath in its sweet scent. Maura eyes widened in surprise and she felt her heart begin to beat faster. His hot breath tickled her neck as he leaned closer to her. Afraid that he might hear the rapid pounding beneath her chest she turned abruptly and began to sprint towards her home.

Rain was now coming down in sheets and bouncing back up from the ground hitting her shins almost painfully. A small copse of trees was nearby so she quickly changed direction and headed towards them, darting underneath. Running close behind her Ciar followed her under the trees and both of them stood there while catching their breath.

Sheltered by the trees but not by the wind Ciar automatically stepped closer to Maura and before she could turn from him again, pulled her into his arms. Maura trapped with no escape felt her heart pounding harder and was certain he must now feel it. Ciar relaxed his arms slightly as he was worried that she would feel his own heart, which hammered beneath his skin. Gently he placed a kiss on the top of her head. Shocked by the tender feel of his lips she looked up sharply, nearly butting his jaw and could not help the small chuckle that escaped. Releasing her to rub his chin he looked sternly down at her and she quickly shut her mouth. That is better...he thought. Too late she noticed the merriment in his eyes as he bent his head swiftly this time to place his lip on her own. Her eyes fluttered shut as he continued to explore her soft mouth with his. Caught in a rare moment of blissful surrender she stood up on her tiptoes and returned his kiss with fiery abandon. Ciar nearly broke away in stunned awareness but his body overruled his thoughts and he returned her passion with an unrelenting fierceness. Briefly, Maura opened her eyes and seeing Ciar so close eventually brought her crashing back to the present. Struggling to free herself from his grip she twisted her mouth away from his and Ciar could do nothing except release her. She opened her mouth to speak, but no words would come so she gathered her skirts and ran towards the croft she shared with her mother. Ciar mesmerised by the soft parting of her lips as she went to speak touched his own and was too late to stop her from fleeing...

He woke, still dressed and dishevelled. Oh no...he thought. It simply defied logic...it quite simply could not be...

CHAPTER FOURTEEN

After Adam had dropped Melissa back to Fairwinds she ran up the steps with a huge smile on her face, feeling gloriously happy and content. She could not wait to tell Suzy what had happened at lunch. He had been the perfect gentleman. They had talked about all of their varied interests. It had actually surprised her to find out that Adam was a keen sailor, something that she had always wanted to try. He had even offered to take her away somewhere and charter a yacht. He made it sound so easy and fun and she did not miss the romantic subtly he used to persuade her.

She finally felt hope for her future and could not mistake the tingly feeling she felt inside whenever she now thought of Adam. Each new revelation that he revealed about himself warmed her to him even more. She hadn't realised that they shared so many things in common. How very different he was now, having matured a great deal. His humour and wit were still as quick as ever and she could not help but notice that he had filled out rather nicely too. He was always making her laugh with his quips and funny little stories and she truly believed that life with him could be full of love and never dull. She breathed a contented sigh and hanging her coat up she went to find Suzy. She knew Suzy was still here as her car was still parked outside on the drive, but when she called there was no answer.

Suzy did in fact hear Melissa calling her but had remained seated on her suitcase rehearsing what she would say and how, ever since Melissa had left earlier. She decided that she would just have to do it and stopped worrying how it might come out. Only two things worried her. One was that she did not want to sound desperate, although glancing down at her case she thought that it might be too late for that! Two, what if Melissa said no? No, that could not happen and Suzy was not going to let that happen. Counting to ten, she took a deep breath then shouted out to Melissa.

In the kitchen, Melissa heard Suzy call and thought she must have been taking a nap. Racing up the staircase she burst into Suzy's room and then halted abruptly at the door. The smile vanished from her lips.

" What are you doing? You're not going, are you?" Melissa struggled to say in a mere whisper.

"Er...you mean this?" Suzy said pointing to her case beneath her, with slightly stooped shoulders and a lopsided smile.

"Yes that. I mean...were you going to go and not say goodbye?"

"No...no it's nothing like that." Suzy smiled reassuringly.

Melissa relaxed, for a moment all the elation she had felt since her lunch with Adam nearly vanished. She was not ready for Suzy to go, not yet anyway. Relieved but puzzled as to why Suzy had packed her case she asked her again why?

Suzy swallowed audibly and shrugged her shoulders. Then feeling a little more confident stood up, well slipped of the case awkwardly and luckily landed on her feet on the floor in front of the bed. Straightening her back she answered Melissa.

"I think we should go to Scotland, today as a matter of fact. It is high time you got out of this house for a few days at least and had some fun. Just think, it would be great, a sort of adventure if you like." There she had said it. It was nothing like what she had rehearsed but she was proud of the way she had delivered it in an almost prime ministerial fashion and with no cock-ups. Hands on hips she looked at Melissa pleadingly but firmly.

Melissa was dumbstruck. Yes they had talked about going to Scotland, mainly so she could take a look at one of the other estates, but for Suzy to have packed and stand there so adamantly, she was sure that there was more to this than she was letting on. Deciding to let it go for now, she stood thinking for a moment, looking down at the floor. She did say to Suzy a few days ago that they could go after she had signed the paperwork, briefly thinking about Mr Mackenzie, made her blush slightly and she quickly pushed him out of her mind. Maybe the further away she was from him then the quicker she could forget how awfully, embarrassingly she had acted in his office. Then there was Adam. She had arranged to meet him again for lunch tomorrow. She could not possibly let him down. It just was not in her nature, besides she wanted to see him again. They were going to take the horses out and she was going to surprise him by bringing along a picnic. There was not going to be much sunny weather left, now so close to October and she wanted to make the most of it. What better time was there for a picnic down by the river. Looking up at Suzy again, she noticed that she had not moved, did not even think she had breathed while waiting for her to answer. Then again, she thought, what better time was there to go to Scotland. Fleetingly she thought back to Mr Mackenzie and the painting she saw in his office.

Remembering the beauty of it, she recalled thinking at that moment, that it must have been painted around this time of year, she remembered the colours being vividly warm shades of Autumn and a slow smile spread across her lips and her eyes twinkled that decided it for her. If Suzy had been looking at Melissa's pendant she would have seen that twinkle too, but had concentrated instead on Melissa's face. As soon as she saw her smiling, she knew Melissa had made her mind up to go. Relief flooded through her and with no words needed, she walked over to Melissa and gave her a squeeze. As Suzy practically crushed her in a friendly embrace she did also think that it would be a nice thank you present to Suzy for taking the time out to be with her at this time and she definitely felt there was something that Suzy was not telling her. Her last thought was of Adam. She could always see Adam when she returned, could not she?

Eager to tell Suzy about her lunch with Adam, she suddenly thought it was strange that Suzy had not in fact asked her about it herself. Just as she was about to mention it, Suzy grabbed her arm and started leading her down the landing to her own room. With a flourish, Suzy pulled open the wardrobe doors and started to select dresses, trousers and jumpers from inside. Sounding innocent, despite the feeling of dread that Melissa would change her mind, Suzy asked where she kept her suitcase and all Melissa could do was point to a second door, which housed a cupboard. Suzy strutted over to the cupboard and after rummaging around, found the case tucked away and hidden at the very back. Pulling it out she dragged it over to Melissa, who by now was sitting on the bed and opened it with a flourish.

"There you go, I'll be back in a jiffy!" she said as she rushed out of the bedroom. Once she reached her own room she entered and shut the door behind her and stayed leaning across the doorway. Taking a deep breath she was momentarily astounded that Melissa had agreed so quickly, instead of the usual debate. Well she was not about to let Melissa change her mind, not now and thanked God for small mercies. Promising him that from now on, she would not be so frivolous. Would stick with only one guy at a time and attempt a Sunday service at least once in her life. Fleetingly she thought maybe she had promised too much and quickly amended it to just the Sunday service. Feeling much better she opened the door again and rushed back into Melissa's room. When she got there she thanked God again as she saw Melissa had already started to put her clothes inside the case.

When she had finished, Melissa dragged her case out of the room and down the landing, while Suzy ran to her own room to collect hers. The two of them had talked animatedly about Scotland throughout and continued to do so, as they made their way downstairs. It was not until they reached the bottom that Suzy suddenly remembered the most important part of the trip. How were they to get there! Not wanting to alarm Melissa she casually turned to her and suggested that it might be a good idea for Melissa to phone ahead and let the staff know that they would be there either later today or tomorrow. Melissa agreed and went into the library meanwhile Suzy ran into the lounge and grabbed her mobile from her bag. When she got through to the airline, she booked two seats, which left early that evening. Just as she tucked her mobile away Melissa joined her in the lounge and Suzy told her they were all set, having just enough time to make it to the airport.

Adam entered Langford's rubbing his hand together in triumph. She was falling for him. He could persuade her to marry him now, he was so confident... but no, he still had time, three weeks left until Winchester called in his debt and he was not worried one bit. It could now be paid in full, then he would plot his revenge. Mrs Betts noticed Adam as he came in and stopped dusting the antique ornaments on the sideboard. She had to admit he seemed full of the joys of spring and wondered where he'd been. As he went to walk straight past her without so much as curt nod, she stepped into his path.

"Afternoon Master Donnell, a pleasant one too, wouldn't you say?"

He looked down his nose at her and smiled sinisterly. "Yes Mrs Betts, I do believe it is."

She stepped back out of his way as though pushed and he carried on through the hall and down towards his private office. She watched him as he removed a key and let himself in without any further acknowledgement. The smile he gave her made her shudder as before and she thought he spoke with an undisguised trace of sadistic satisfaction. What had changed that boy, she would never know. He might have been spoilt and sulky, but never would she have imagined he would turn cold towards her, despite her remaining wary of him at times. During the last couple of years he had become more and more secretive and particularly in the last six months, when he had disappeared, no word of his whereabouts for nearly three or four months and with no explanation as to why, he had begun to act strangely. She could not quite put her finger on it, all she knew was that he frightened her more and more of late, with his strange behaviour and the look he sometimes had in his eyes. Turning abruptly she carried on dusting with a renewed energy, praying that something good would happen to that boy, maybe then she'd stop feeling nervous around him.

Adam stepped into his private office and clicked the door shut softly behind him, locking the door from the inside and putting the key back into his pocket. No one, except him had access to this room. He walked over to an original Victorian, kidney shaped, solid mahogany drinks cabinet and poured himself a large whisky, caressing the warm, smooth, glossy texture of the wood. He loved the feel of it under his fingertips and then his thoughts turned to Melissa and running his hand against her warm, smooth body. Finishing his drink in one mouthful, he put the glass down lovingly on the surface and went over to sit at his desk. He was never without Melissa. She occupied every waking minute and interrupted his sleep too. She was going to be his ultimate prize. Ridding himself of his dimwit parents to inherit the house was not enough. Through gambling debts, loans and women he had had to mortgage the house just to keep him alive. Money was now running out. Then there was Winchester. Adam relaxed a little no longer fearful of him. Soon, much sooner than he dared dreamed, Melissa would be his and along with it her inheritance. As well as paying his debt to him, Adam had also planned a little surprise. As thoughts of Melissa and revenge started to thrum through his veins he lounged back in the chair, letting the whiskey, which was now warming his stomach, lull him into a state of false contentment. She had agreed to see him again tomorrow. For him it could not come quickly enough. Maybe he ought to ring her, women loved that sort of thing, so sitting forward he reached for the phone and dialled her number.

After several rings he heard the dreary dull voice of her butler down the line.

"It's Adam, could you please tell Melissa I wish to have a quick word with her...please." He hated having to sound meek, but he was too close now to want to cause any misgivings, especially with her staff.

"Good Evening Master Donnell. I am afraid I cannot help you sir. You see she left a note, excuse me one moment."

Adam heard a kerfuffle in the background and tapped his foot impatiently, wondering where the hell she was.

"Ah...I do apologise Sir, I have the note here. Lets see, ah yes, she has gone with Miss Suzy to Scotland..."

Adam did not hear the rest of the note as he sat there in angry disbelief, a thousand possible explanations running through his head. He must go there... Tonight... He had not come so close as to have that pathetic meddling do-gooder

Suzy spoil his plans. She would regret taking Melissa away from him. It would not be difficult to get rid of her and have Melissa all to himself.

"It is quite alright." He just about managed to say, disguising his increasingly bitter rage. Slamming down the receiver, he got up and started to pace up and down. He quickly thought about what he would need to take with him and without any further hesitation he picked the phone up again and booked the first available flight. His outrage was threatening his control. A young girl with a squeaky, high-pitched voice answered and politely informed him that the first available flight would not be until six thirty the following morning. Gripping the receiver tightly, he spoke through clenched teeth and secured a seat. Instead of replacing it, he threw it across the room with so much force that it ricocheted across the parquet floor and landed unplugged from the wall. His face twisted with anger and his body tense with suppressed rage made him swear that Suzy would suffer for this. Her fate was now his. Pouring another whiskey, he sipped it slowly this time, trying to calm the demons that were infesting his body. For two hours he sat in silence, darkness his only companion. Not once did he move. Not even to finish his drink. Only his mind remained active. Eventually he rose from the chair and picked the phone up from the floor, replacing it on his desk. Then he took the key out of his pocket and unlocked the door. Every movement he made was strained and slow. His inner demons had tasted freedom and did not want to lay quietly. Shutting the door, he locked it securely and gripped the key so tightly in his hand a small trickle of blood escaped, leaving an undetectable trail on the polished floor as he made his way to his room.

CHAPTER FIFTEEN

Melissa and Suzy arrived in Scotland and after collecting their luggage went to a car rental desk to inquire about a suitable car for the next few days. Night had already fallen and as neither of them knew exactly how to get to the highlands from the airport, decided to wait until the morning. So after arranging to pick the car up first thing, they then decided to stay in a hotel close to the airport that night.

"Wow! We really made it, did we not." Suzy exclaimed, as they made their way out of the airport and boarded a shuttle to take them to the nearest hotel.

"Yes, we did Suzy. To tell you the truth I am actually a little surprised at myself." Melissa replied not exactly feeling the same kind of excitement as Suzy, but feeling strange nevertheless.

"Tomorrow the real adventure begins! I'm not going to be able to sleep." Suzy turned to Melissa as the bus halted outside the hotel. She hoped that if she could keep her away from Adam for a time then maybe she begin to come to her senses about him.

They entered the hotel hoping there would be a room available. The receptionist, although well groomed, remind Suzy of Cinderella's wicked step-mother as she looked down at them, then at her computer screen. With a not so apologetic look she told them that they were fully booked. As they picked up their cases and started to walk away, the receptionist suddenly called out to them, unable to hide her surprise.

"It appears we do have a room after all. A cancellation has just flashed up on my screen." The receptionist did not add that she had never in all her years, seen a cancellation come at such an opportune time.

"That is great! Thank you, we'll take it." Suzy said in a hurry. After paying they were shown to their room and ordered a light snack, having already eaten on the plane. Suzy, excitedly, continued to chat about all the things they could do while they were there and of all the places they could go and visit, while Melissa remained silent, thinking about Adam and wishing she had at least told him she would be away for a few days. It seemed only a few minutes later that an assortment of sandwiches, tea, coffee and biscuits arrived and while they sat on the opposite beds eating, they poured over the tourist maps Suzy had picked up from the rental office and the hotel reception, picking out a scenic route that would take them along and up through the Western Isles. After getting ready for bed, Suzy turned out the bedside lamp and fell quickly into a deep sleep. Melissa laid in the darkness her mind unable to rest as easily as Suzy's. Guilty thoughts of leaving Adam with no word and surprise at herself for making the journey here and puzzlement about Suzy wanting to leave so quickly prevented her from sleeping. She turned on her side and held the pendant, still around her neck, in her hand, willing herself to sleep. As she began to doze her last thought was of the painting she had seen in Mr Mackenzie's office.

..."Ye came", he whispered softly, using the soft burr he knew sent shivers down her spine, in her hair, after he lifted her from the horse and slid her body down his own, only to crush her lips when they were level. Breathlessly she stood back and while trying to steady her wildly beating heart she habitually looked all around to make sure she had not been followed. Catching her chin in his palm as she turned her head, he looked down at her with a sensuously crooked grin and brought her face up to his once more. Standing on tiptoes, for he was now a foot taller than she, she matched the passion in his kiss with her own. They did not separate this time until the proud stallion that stood nearby let out a loud snort and ground his hoof into the ground. At once they turned to the horse and then to each other and burst out laughing.

"Twad seim Thor be impatient." Conrad chuckled. "Come Maura, I want tae show ye something." He removed Thor's reins so he could wander freely and then reached for Maura's hand pulling her behind the huge oak tree and ravished her mouth once more before letting her go reluctantly.

In the distance hidden by a copse of trees a man sat on horseback and stared intently at the two figures as they chased each other round the tree. His eyes were piercing and unrelenting as he focused on the woman. Finally he had found her, for he would never forget seeing such a beauty. Even from this distance he noticed her lush curves through the near threadbare dress she wore. Shifting uncomfortably in his saddle he felt the familiar stirrings of desire as he watched unseen. His whole body became at once alert and taut as he narrowed his gaze. He guided his horse around the tree in front of him and used the next one to hide himself better. She raised her face to the sun and then as though she had sensed his movements, turned abruptly to where he was mounted. Seized by lust, his blood roared through his veins so loudly it was deafening to his ears as he clearly made out her face. No breath escaped his lips as he waited to see if he'd been seen. Then he exhaled slowly as he saw the man reach for her once more and tumble her to the ground. With a hunters grace he edged his horse backwards, silently never taking his eyes off his prey and this time when he exhaled he turned his horse abruptly and rode hard back across the land from where he'd come, his blood still roaring in his ears...

Melissa blinked and then blinked again as she focused on her surroundings. Remembering where she was she looked over to where Suzy lay and felt a small measure of comfort seeing her there. She stared up towards the ceiling, wishing she could remember what she must have been dreaming about and why it would have wakened her. A pair of twinkling eyes remained, then disappeared from her minds eye. Blowing a stray hair from her eyes, she twiddled with the bed covers. Maybe, it was just all the stress of recent weeks causing the many sleepless nights she was having more often than not. Sighing deeply, she was glad for a moment she could not remember any details in case the images were more terrifying than the ones that popped in to her head unbidden throughout the day, of what must have been her mother's last moments. Turning on her side she closed her eyes once more and fought her mind to keep the images away. A small smile touched her lips as Conrad's face appeared in her minds eye but vanished as quickly as it came, replaced by one of Adam.

Suzy eyed Melissa curiously as the sun peaked through the blinds announcing it was time to get up. As she was still sound asleep curled up like a baby covered by a single sheet. The rest of them were in such disarray it was as though she had been in a fight with them. Getting up slowly she walked to the window and opened the blinds wider. She smiled to herself at the brilliant blue sky and warmth of the sun then went into the bathroom to have a shower. Melissa woke for the second time bathed in light and to the sound of Suzy singing dreadfully in the shower. Groaning, she stretched her full length then got up to look out of the window, just as Suzy had done. Still singing and what Melissa thought, trying her hardest to do! Suzy came back into the room smiling at Melissa now that she was up and had her back to her.

"It looks absolutely glorious out there does it not?" Suzy quipped enthusiastically.

"Don't be fooled by the sun Suzy" Melissa chuckled and turned to face her. "It can still be cold despite the cloudless sky. It often is at this time of year."

Suzy looked at Melissa questioningly.

"And how exactly would you know that, you've never been here before?" Slightly taken aback by the look on Suzy's face, Melissa smiled warmly and at the same time felt the beginnings of a tingly sensation in her stomach. Looking away, she rested her hands lightly on the windowsill and let her gaze search the sky, before speaking again.

"I'm not sure, perhaps I have been here before and can't remember." The laughter suddenly died on her lips as she felt as though someone had placed a hot poker to her chest. Automatically her hand sought the pendant and she felt the heat consume her hand and travel the length of her arm. Letting go abruptly she turned to face Suzy and saw that her expression mirrored her own.

"Are you alright? You've gone as white as a sheet." Concerned, Suzy, walked over to Melissa and put an arm around her, walking her back to the bed she sat her down. After a moment, Melissa told her she felt fine and got up to go to the bathroom, leaving Suzy staring after her.

Melissa stared at her reflection in the mirror and touched her pendant. Strange sensations assailed her and stirred wildly in Melissa's stomach. As she contemplated the reflection staring back at her, she felt all at once at home but also lost and she shook her head as if she was being silly for thinking like that. Taking a deep breath, she finished up in the bathroom and went back out to join Suzy who had just finished packing.

Both lost in their own thoughts they left the room and went back to the reception area of the hotel. Melissa smiled as a pretty, young girl who was much more of a Cinderella than the previous ugly sister receptionist was there to greet them. The young girl smiled in return and wished them good morning whilst handing them the keys to the hire car that had arrived only moments ago. When Melissa took the keys from the young receptionist, she had a questioning look on her face. Smiling brightly the young receptionist explained that the hire car company had decided to drop the car to the hotel so they would not be delayed in their journey North.

"Oh!" Melissa exclaimed... "That was kind of them."

After checking out Melissa and Suzy left the hotel and got into the car. At precisely the same moment Suzy and Melissa turned to look at one another, the young receptionist stepped outside to wave them off, neither

Melissa or Suzy noticed an almond shaped bright eyed cat, wrap itself around the legs of the receptionist.

Suzy unfolded the map that she still had in her hand and doing her very best impression of a queen in a bygone era pointed forwards and in typical Suzy fashion told Melissa to start the engine and be off!

As they left the hotel behind and began the journey north, the city began to get smaller whilst the space around them seemed to get larger. Making their way towards the Highlands they both chatted about what might lay ahead and in a rare moment of silence, each of them contemplated the two men at the fore front of their minds...Conrad Mackenzie and Adam Donnell.

CHAPTER SIXTEEN

The drive out of Edinburgh did not take as long as Melissa had first thought, who had decided to take the wheel first. Suzy sat looking out of the window at the passing scenery not quite believing that they had actually made it this far and despite having occasional misgivings and a feeling of something she couldn't quite put her finger on, felt an unwavering force driving her to protect Melissa.

On the open road they passed by majestic mountains and lochs, which beckoned the passer-by to stop and just stare in awe at the scene laid out before them... Suzy sighed in contentment, causing Melissa to look over at her and smile warmly...

"It's beautiful isn't it?" Melissa spoke reverently, not wishing to break the spell.

"Its magical Melissa.... why has it taken this long to visit?" Suzy pried her gaze away from the car window to look at Melissa.

"Hey... lets just stop and soak it in..." Suzy said wistfully.

"Ok", Melissa replied with a smile of her own and a deep sigh of an inexplicable feeling of belonging.

Melissa drove for a few more miles looking for somewhere safe to stop at the side of the road and just as they approached the Glencoe pass, Melissa found a safe place to park up to get out and stare in wonder at the scenery before them.

Mountains stood towering and proud on either side of the road, giving Melissa and Suzy a feeling of being trapped in a lost place and time. The beauty of each mountain left you breathless and as each cloud passed over the sun, the mountains took on a foretelling look of a thousand tales and the heather swaying in the breeze almost echoed the whispers of past battles and bloodshed. Melissa felt a shiver and could hear the screams of those that were slayed. Spying Suzy just off in the distance exploring she shut her eyes briefly and felt for the pendant around her neck seeking comfort. For the first time there was none. Blinking rapidly she tried to clear the images and sounds that started to crowd her thoughts.... Then as she abruptly let go of the pendant upon hearing Suzy call, the images and whispers faded. Turning to where Suzy stood, she breathed deeply and longingly while staring up at the surrounding mountains and made her way over to her.

"Hey Melissa...look over there..." Melissa stood shielding her eyes from the sun and looked in the direction that Suzy was pointing. Off in the distance the sun glistened on the surface of a small stream that wound its way around the base of the mountain and out into a Loch. Purple and pink hues of wild heather caressed the land spread out before them.

"Beautiful..." Suzy said with a sigh

"Yes Suzy" Melissa replied with an air of melancholy, as she felt a great sadness wash over her despite the rugged beauty surrounding her.

"Are you ok?" Suzy asked as she reluctantly peeled her gaze away from the scenery to turn and face Melissa.

"I think so? Although I cannot seem to shake a feeling that I cannot even put into words. I just...just...oh I don't know, it's nothing ha." A slight nervous giggle escaped Melissa, however Suzy didn't seem convinced and found it odd that they both seemed to have feelings neither of whom could explain, let alone talk about without sounding stupid...or mad. For as Suzy had stared into the distance, following the stream with he eyes, she too found it difficult to put into words how being here made her feel.

"Come on..." Suzy said with an enthusiasm she no longer felt, "lets get moving".

Silently they both made their way back to the car and after taking one last look at the magnificent beauty before them, got into the car and drove off.

After an hour they decided to pull over a have another break, neither of them being able to get enough of the passing scenery. As they reached a small village called Invergarry they pulled over at a hotel, that stood isolated on the banks of a river but as it seemed to be the only one around they went in for a much needed toilet stop and coffee.

Once refreshed the two of them sat on a bench outside the hotel, admiring the peacefulness and tranquillity of the surrounding landscape. Melissa felt slightly restless as they were still an hour or so away from her parents estate in Scotland, she got up and told Suzy she would just be a few minutes and took off over the bridge and down a small path that ran alongside the waters edge. Alone and tired Melissa kept putting one foot in front of the other, not really paying attention to how far she was going or how long she had been gone for. Surrounded by woodland, Melissa at last looked up to see that the path she had been following opened up to reveal a beautiful house and just beyond the house stood the ruins of a castle. Suddenly, thinking she had trespassed she grabbed the pendent in exclamation and squeezed her eyes shut for the pain came swiftly and unexpectedly, trapping her in a vortex of spiralling agony...she tried calling out but her voice was cut off and lost in the swirling voices, pushing at her mind, her body felt as though a thousand hands were grabbing her pulling and pushing her... she tried to open her eyes but it was as though someone was there blinding her....with every fearful breath she took she willed herself to scream and at the same time her eyes were released by their hold, the scream died in her throat..as through the chaos in her mind she heard her name...but it wasn't her name...was it? Blinking rapidly, her gaze swung to a pair of eyes that were looking out of the trees and she swallowed audibly...it couldn't be she thought and as she took a step forward, he vanished and Melissa felt as though her body had just been spat out of the vortex that was holding her prisoner. Spinning around to Suzy shouting her name, she took one last look at the castle ruin and of the woodland surrounding the path and could swear that those eyes were still watching her.

Wha in gods neam was Maura doing here? Ciar fleeting thought about what she was wearing but was so shocked to see her, that he automatically called to her as he stood up abruptly from crouching low hiding amongst the trees near to Macdonnells stronghold, narrowly missing a low branch. After looking heavenwards and thanking god for not having his young life cut short he stood transfixed staring at Maura, shaking his head in bewilderment at her stupidity... he knew she was a headstrong lass and was nearly always courting danger but to venture out this far onto MacDonnells land... indeed near up to the stronghold. Remembering that's where he was himself, he crouched low again and just as quickly as the thought entered his head she disappeared. Rubbing his eyes he stared at where she had just a moment ago stood for all the world like she didn't know where she was and then pinched himself to make sure no one was playing tricks. Wha kind of witchery hae the Macdonnells gate up thair sleeves...Ciar almost said aloud. Just beyond earshot he spied two men walking in his direction, both of them looked as though they had suddenly stopped as if something had caught their attention. Ciar's gaze swung back to where Maura had stood moments ago and then did not breath as the two men intent on reaching the exact same spot purposefully strode towards where she had stood. As silent as a predator Ciar shrank back amongst the growth, hidden from view and laid low daring not to breath as he listened to the two men.

"Did ye sie that Alpin? Breac spoke whilst trying to keep the disbelief from his voice.

"Aye mi friend, that I did...' Alpin responded thoughtfully. In his mind he still saw the woman stood there in the strangest clothes he had ever seen but it was her face that stayed with him. Her dark hair looked to be piled on top of her head with loose strands that fell around her face, just begging for him to take between his fingers. As lust filled his blood he felt himself stir in his breeches and slapped Breac on the back.

"Well mi freend, noo thair be a lass who hasna had the pleasure of mi company'...for I nae be forgetting that one!" Alpin chuckled, still picturing her face and the strange expression he thought he saw on it. Although he and Breac were a little distance away from where they now stood. There was no mistaking the way her expression changed when he and Braec stepped into view. As he glanced around him, he saw and heard nothing but couldn't be sure if she had indeed been looking at them or through the woods to his left. With one last glance around and Breac chiding him for having missed an opportunity to grab the wench, he shrugged his shoulders and thinking that he would indeed find her and bed her, returned with Breac to the castle, unable to remove the vision from his thoughts.

Ciar clenched and unclenched his fist imagining its grip held that of the man who spoke and waited until they had disappeared from around the corner from where they had come before he slowly but silently retreated further into the woods until he was back at the clearing where he had left his horse. On the ride back to Mackenzie land he mulled over all that he had learnt' and had much to tell his laird regarding the enemy, he swore under his breath that soon the Mackenzies will have justice, everything is falling into place.

Suzy watched Melissa disappear over the bridge until she lost sight of her. Crossing and uncrossing her legs she got up and sat down again on the bench, she instinctively wanted to follow Melissa but had agreed to give her a few minutes, taking a deep breath she wondered why she felt so on edge, after all nothing could possibly happen all the way up here. Unable to shake the feeling of trepidation and repeatedly looking at her watch, expecting Melissa to appear on the bridge at any minute, gave up and decided to see where Melissa could have got too. Suzy wasn't immune to the surrounding landscape and momentarily lost herself in whimsical fantasies of a strapping highlander, who just at that moment came running towards her out of the forest in nothing but leather thigh hugging trousers, muscles flexing and long hair flying behind him. She took a shuddering breath as in her minds eye her fantasy continued with him coming to an abrupt halt in front of her and without asking for permission he grabbed hold of her roughly, but without hurting her and while pulling her towards him he lowered his head...

"Ouch!" Suzy exclaimed while holding her head and looking up... An owl, after twisting its head in a full circle hooted at her and she swore that it winked at her before it flew off... cursing at the owl for dislodging a twig that just so happened to hit her on the head right at the moment she was about to get thoroughly kissed by the most horniest man her imagination had come up with to date, was not amused! 'Humph...' Suzy breathed grumpily and looking down the path that Melissa had taken and still not seeing any sign that she was on her way back, took a moment to picture the strapping highlander in her mind and storing it for a rainy day, wondered if men like that existed anymore or whether they were just resigned to overactive imaginations like hers; carried on following the path looking for Melissa.

As she approached the same clearing that Melissa had reached some minutes before, she caught Melissa staring into the forest standing stock still and not breathing.

"Melissa?" Suzy shouted. "Are you ok?" When Melissa still didn't turn around, Suzy's instinct took over. Looking over to the same spot that Melissa seemed to not be able to take her eyes from, she approached slowly not wanting to startle her and then taking her hand she whispered "it's ok..."

"It was him...'" she whispered..."it was him..." Melissa repeated, still unable to take her eyes from the side of the forest.

"Who Melissa...who was it?" Suzy asked tentatively.

"Ciar..."

Suzy looked at `Melissa's face then over to the spot that Melissa was staring at and couldn't see anyone.

"There's no-one there Mel" Suzy stated worryingly...

"He was there...I...I...saw him..." Melissa turned abruptly to Suzy. For a minute Suzy wondered if she wasn't the only one to have an overactive imagination, as she had no idea who Melissa was going on about.

"Saw who? Who is Ciar?" Suzy asked perplexed.

"I don't know Suzy... I have no idea... but I felt as though I should... I don't feel so good would you take over the driving?" Melissa pleaded while her head felt like it was about to splinter into several pieces.

"Of course....come on, let's go..." Suzy led Melissa away and back to the car and looking back it was then she noticed the castle ruin and gave an involuntary shudder, taking one last look at the forest she guided Melissa back to car, all thoughts of Ciar, whoever he was and of her imaginary highlander gone as she worried about getting them both to the car and to Caberfeidh before dark.

Neither of them noticed the owl sitting on a branch high above them or the pendant that glowed softly around Melissa's neck when she locked eyes with the eyes that stared at her from the forest.

CHAPTER SEVENTEEN

Adam reached the airport and as he approached the check in desk he didn't notice the way people moved out of his way, barely controlling his movements and his face from showing the twisting, bitter rage that he still felt inside, he dropped his bag at the desk and pushed his hands through his hair and giving the check-in girl a suggestively, seductive smile, making her blush, which instantly had a soothing effect on Adam and at last breathing normally he managed to confirm his flight details and get his boarding pass.

As he waited around to board, his mind kept going over the last time he saw Melissa, to see if he could pin-point what could have possibly made her go to Scotland tonight, when he had only been with her a few hours previously at lunch where he was sure he was winning her over, talking about old times and laughing together...he was his usual charming self, witty and amusing and she seemed to be so happy when he dropped her off.

Suzy...it had to be...he thought to himself as he clenched and unclenched his fist. That meddling do-gooder... Just the thought of Suzy made his skin crawl, he really needed to get rid of her, she could spoil everything and he was getting closer, he could almost taste it... An image of the solicitor dealing with Melissa's estate came from nowhere, unbidden and instantly sent an icy chill down Adam's spine. Humph...Adam thought... What was his name?... Mackenzie? Well if Melissa and that bitch didn't stop going on about him then he would have to do something about him too...An ugly smile crossed Adams lips.. Not before that MacKenzie fellow had Melissa sign for her all that was now hers... and soon to be his... A sneeringly sinister laugh escaped Adams lips and he tightened his grip on his boarding pass.

Melissa hadn't said a word since they both got back in the car and set off for the final leg of the journey towards Caberfeidh. Suzy thought back to where Melissa had stood at the castle ruins, staring motionless into the surrounding woods. Ciar... was the name she whispered but who the hell was Ciar? Suzy thought... Looking across at Melissa she was loath to break the silence, as Melissa looked as though she was a thousand years away. Gripping the steering wheel tighter and no longer exclaiming about the passing rugged beauty, her mind wrestled with an assortment of thoughts, images and feelings. What was going on? Suzy thought...Ever since Melissa's mother had passed away, there seemed to be a lot of weird shit going on... Thinking back to when she first got that phone call from Melissa, she had felt the hairs on the back of her neck rise and had a bad case of the heebie-jeebies. She didn't expect Melissa to be herself what with all she had to do regarding her mothers death, such as sort out the estates...estates holy shit....Melissa's parents hardly mentioned them at all! Melissa now had three to sort out... why would her parents hardly mention them? Suzy couldn't even remember a time when they spoke about them...only spoke about 'the other property' now and again...not estates! Suzy's mind continued to drift...That sexily scrummy solicitor also mentioned some belongings In a vault? Melissa seemed to have no idea what those things could be or what they would have had hidden away? As each day goes past, there seems to be more questions raised? Suzy grunted under her breath and quickly looked across to Melissa, who was sitting as still as a rock, silent, staring straight out at the road in front, except for an occasional breath. Turning back to the road herself, Suzy began thinking about Adam... an icy shiver went down her back, making her toes curl, and she instinctively gripped the steering wheel tighter. She remembered the way he looked at Melissa at dinner the other day...why the sudden interest in Melissa..okay, Adam had always had a soft spot for Melissa but he was a nasty piece of work and Suzy refused to let the memories of what he did to her surface. Squashing them to the back of her mind she thought again about Adam's interest in Melissa. She couldn't quite put her finger on it, but something inside of her was telling her it wasn't a good thing.

Letting out a sigh, Suzy glanced out of the window at the seemingly endless beauty that didn't seem to change, they couldn't be that far away now and briefly she glanced at her watch for confirmation. Letting her mind drift again she chanced another look at Melissa, who hadn't moved...Suzy wondered if Melissa had actually stopped breathing or was lost in some sort of time warp, looking out at the road in front she thought about what could possibly be in the vault that was so valuable and why did Melissa know nothing about it? Something kept pulling at the corners of her mind but she was at a loss as to what she was supposed to think... Although Suzy admitted to herself that she was a little curious... okay really curious as to what was in there, she also knew that Melissa wasn't her normal self and it wasn't just down to the fact she had recently lost her mother. No Suzy thought, it was more that that, much more and even if she couldn't quite put her fingers on it now, she was sure it would come to her at some point.

As Suzy turned into the wooded, lone, dark, desolate road that would lead them to Caberfeidh, Melissa seemed to come alive and she turned to Suzy, exclaiming at a group of trees, whose bark had an unnatural looking white/silver colour that glistened in the fading light and which stood tall and proud amongst a bed of the most vibrant purple flowers either of them had seen, it was almost magical. The surrounding trees had a rich dark brown bark and the purple flowers seemed less vibrant and almost lacking. The group of trees, almost in acknowledgement of their appreciative visitors, whispered to each other, like they had done hundreds of years before.

"This is the first time I have ever been here Suzy...yet It feels...it feels as though I was mean't to come" Melissa stated quietly and questioningly.

"Well of course you were mean't to come Melissa, the estate has been left to you?" Suzy replied, trying to lighten the sombreness in the car. However Suzy also felt that somehow they were both meant to be here.

The woodland eventually gave way to an open meadow and both Melissa and Suzy sat forward in their seats as they glimpsed water from the loch glistening in the fading sunlight against a backdrop of hills and pine trees that went beyond what the eye could see. As they rounded the bend in the drive Caberfeidh finally came into view, causing Suzy to come to an emergency stop.

Caberfeidh simply took Melissa's and Suzy's breath away. It was now an exquisite baronial manor house that had two turrets, although different heights, both were reaching towards the sky and joined together by an imposing facade of pale stone with an abundance of windows. Behind one of the turrets a square tower stood, slightly taller and as a testament to the original castle that had once stood here.

As Suzy drove the remaining short distance to the entrance. A woman and a young boy game out of the main door both with warm friendly faces. Melissa recognised Anna straight away despite having not seen her since she was a child.

"Anna... Anna" Melissa shouted as she got out of the car and ran towards the entrance. "I thought you'd abandoned me all those years ago! You left without saying goodbye and Mother wouldn't even let me breathe your name!!"

Trying not to squeeze the life out of Anna as she hugged her fiercely, Melissa felt the back of her hair being stroked just like she did when she was a child, squeezing her eyes tightly shut she let the feeling of warmth spread through her before breaking the contact and looked at Anna to double check she was real.

"Well now my child, it's been a long time but I knew one day you would come."

CHAPTER EIGHTEEN

She was his equal...It did not matter how many times he thought it...roared with the pain of it...or simply accepted it...he could not change it. He stood alone...Always alone...He could feel but not touch, he could see but had no eyes. He could speak yet had no mouth. The air surrounding him crackled with unspent energy. Until he sneered into the empty space, sending small flurries of mist in different directions when he realised it was his own energy that crackled. It had been a long time, which was ironic he thought as time was not something he thought about very often. Time was for those who had but the briefest of moments within a realm. Even the Fey, which he watched sometimes while he walked amongst them, had just a brief moment within the realms. As much as they might like to think otherwise. He kept a vague notion of which century it was and in some instances what year it was. Yet time...time was irrelevant to him, except for when the light magic drew him to her.

The eve before each birth he would feel the beginnings of a subtle shift until it consumed the space he existed in. Unbearably pure, innocent and full off love. It was like a poison invading his being. It was how he knew without knowing that it was time. Every ritual was performed the same way at the same time and at the same place. The elders would gather in their spiritual form to channel their power with hers and to give up some of their essence. He could not deny that the moment was indeed rare and precious but had never been able to brake through their protective barrier so effectively and quickly as he did this time. 'Huh...' he spat...

Perhaps the tables were turning...? He thought... Or was she getting weaker...? He materialised into a Fey and just like the Fey he strutted about his space preening and gloating at invisible witnesses, mulling over the different reasons as to why this time it felt different . . No... He thought....He had never been this close...It was very different this time...She thought that he did not know she ventured into the human realm but he knew because he had watched her many times over the years. He saw her subtle meddling and had countered with his own. Although he could not forget she was his equal. It would seem perhaps that she had forgotten, so used to was she the outcome of each birth. In the midst of his thinking he metamorphosed back to his natural form, swapping between what looked like a thick icy dark fog and then a gentle grey mist.

He stopped his energy from circling the surrounding space and took on a human form. He had not done that since the night of the last gathering. The image of her in human form had stayed with him and it was more of a conundrum that he cared to admit and one which he could not and did not want to contemplate. He had seen her in many different guises throughout time including her natural state...Time...he thought once more, why this eve should he be reflecting upon that last gathering. No matter how much he turned it around in his mind or re-created the events of that night in this space. One fragment of that night superseded all others. Fear...Fear drove him, fed his dark energy and his power. It was the never before seen fear that he glimpsed... for the briefest of moments...in her eyes... he saw real fear. She composed herself quickly but it was the expression on her perfectly formed human face that had kept him returning to that night.

Feeling restless and unable to shake her image from his mind he began to murmur ancient words to summon his power and create objects that he had seen when he had ventured between realms. Where there had been an empty infinite space of darkness now appeared solid items. He started with the space beneath his feet and created a floor made of stone, he then waved his arms wide and stone walls sprung up from the ground where he stood in this timeless dimension. Turning he created a window and even a faint breeze that he could feel on his human skin and with a wave of his other hand he created a fire, surrounded by a large stone hearth. A large leather chair was the next object he created which appeared next to the fire together with a writing table in the opposite corner. Walking slowly, testing out the floor beneath his feet, the clip of each footfall sent an echo of thunder around the room. Lessening his step he tried again and this time there was just the gentle thud of his boot which he had fashioned for his feet. Reaching the chair he sat down to admire the boots. He then looked across the room to admire his human form in the mirror that had appeared. Standing abruptly he did not waste time walking but moved with a speed and fluid grace that belied his human form and held the full length mirror in his hands while his gaze penetrated the glass.

He smiled at his reflection forbiddingly and peered deep beyond his reflection through to the human realm. As he focused his attention, he released one side of the mirror without taking his eyes from it and clicking his finger if bored, proceeded to rub his finger and thumb together. A dark vapour of magic began to form between his fingers and started to snake its way up into the air above and around his head, swirling seductively. In an ancient tongue he began to chant softly like a caressing whisper. Luminous white, purple and blue sparks could be seen and heard hissing and crackling in the midst of the swirling dark mist. As the chanting stopped the swirling mass of magic ceased moving and as he stared deep into the depths of the mirror and found what he sought the magic was released and penetrated the glass to find its target. 'Now I have showed my hand for what it truly is'...he whispered conspiratorially just as he shifted back into his natural form and the space around him reverted back to infinite darkness.

CHAPTER NINETEEN

"Good Morning...How may I help you?" The attractive young concierges assistant asked as she approached the slightly portly gentleman who stood in front of the reception desk at the very fashionable Star Residences.

Located in the centre of Edinburgh it was within walking distance of Princes Street, Haymarket and the castle itself. Winchester had his secretary pick it due to it being apartments as opposed to a hotel which suited his purposes perfectly by giving him privacy. Hotels had a way of letting everyone know your business and Winchester did not like anyone knowing his business unless they "became his business.

"Yes" he replied with a slight leer. Brushing off the uncomfortable feeling he was giving her she smiled sweetly and asked for his name.

"Winchester.." He announced in his low gravely voice. Turning back towards one of his employees he gave a nod to indicate they would stay. The concierges assistant made her way behind the desk as the receptionist was busy with another guest and proceeded to look Mr Winchester up on the reservation system. As Mr Winchester returned to face the girl he smirked as he caught the sight of her behind just before it disappeared behind the desk.

"Ah... Here we are Mr Winchester...I have found your reservation. We have you down for just one night. Is that correct?" She was reluctant to look up as she could feel his eyes boring down at her. However Mr Winchester sensing her discomfort stood waiting until the she had no choice but to look up at him. As she tried to shake the creepy feeling he was giving her he leaned in closer and placing his hands on the desk he replied "Yes...although you may call me Winchester and now that I'm here I might just extend my stay for a little while longer...what do you say?" He said with a sneer. Swallowing her rising disgust and wishing the receptionist next to her would hurry up and check in her guest so that she could pass him over and get out from under his scrutiny, she almost sighed with visible relief when she checked and looking at Winchester with a confidence she didn't feel answered him politely.

"I'm very sorry sir but unfortunately we are fully booked."

"Now that is a shame as I was rather enjoying the view" His smile sent a shiver down her spine and she looked across the foyer hoping to catch the eye of the porter who had just appeared. As luck would have it the porter walked over to the desk on seeing the guests checking in and was just about to reach for the receptionists guest luggage, that he raised an eyebrow when the concierges assistant practically ran around the desk to grab his sleeve. Smiling sweetly albeit relieved, she asked for him to show Mr Winchester up to his apartment. Not giving him time to protest she quickly made her escape leaving the porter with Mr Winchester and his companion.

"Right Sir, If you would like to follow me" and with a flourish the porter picked up the small bag, but just as he reached for the briefcase he felt the strong grip of Winchester's companion on his arm and abruptly let go. Not wanting to cause a scene he swallowed back his retort remembering his position and quietly cursed under his breath. Standing up straight he headed towards the stairs and without checking to see if Mr Winchester and his companion were behind him, headed straight for the apartment on the first floor.

As the porter reached the door to the apartment he opened the door using the key card without invitation and entered, still annoyed at the way the man who looked more like a body guard than a travelling companion had grabbed his arm. Walking inside the apartment he put the bag down and placed the key card on the table. Turning to see Mr

Winchester and the brute that grabbed his arm enter the apartment he politely asked if they needed anything else and when the brute said no, he didn't wait around for them to change their mind and hurriedly left the apartment.The so called brute turned to Winchester.

"Where do you want this boss?" he asked referring to the briefcase he had in his hand.

"Just leave it on the table " Winchester replied as he pointed to the coffee table in the modern and well decorated lounge and went to check out the rest of the apartment. The only sounds that could be heard were a small grunt accompanied by an occasional nod to mark his satisfaction at what he saw.

"Hey boss, what do you fancy watching?" He said with a sardonic laugh while holding up a couple of DVD's. Without bothering to respond, Winchester just masked his look of disbelief that he could employee such brainless idiots, however useful they were in other areas with a look that said a very loud no and inspected the apartment. Getting the hint his employee shrugged his shoulders and put the DVD's back.

The lounge was a contrast in colour, mixing creams and dark wood with a sumptuous leather sofa in the centre with a media centre on one side and three large windows on the other which overlooked the street below. The kitchen area was visible from the lounge and accessed by a few steps leading up to it and there was a small separate office area. Winchester went into the first bedroom he came to and went straight to the window to peer down into the street. Well he thought...time was running out for Adam Donnell.

Adam arrived in Edinburgh and stood restlessly outside of the airport. He was here...finally...and still feeling on edge he began cursing the time as he realised that it was too late to hire a car so lighting up a cigarette he paced for a few minutes to gather his thoughts. Inhaling deeply and thankful that not only did he have a packet of cigarettes on him but he had managed to keep hold of his lighter he thought about where to go until morning. He cursed his impulsiveness as he got into a taxi and asked to be dropped off at a hotel in the centre of town. The taxi driver soon got the hint that Adam did not want to make conversation as every time he tried he got no response and so closed the glass separator and left Adam to his own thoughts.

As Adam sat in the back of the taxi mindlessly watching the street lights go by and having no idea how far or how long it would take to get to a hotel. His thoughts drifted towards Melissa as thinking about her always seemed to help calm him and he relaxed back into the seat letting the feeling drift over him. Glad the driver had put the separator up he got out his phone and briefly toyed with the idea of letting her know he was in Scotland. Pressing her number into his phone he waited...one...two..three rings and then abruptly disconnected the call. Suzy was with her, how could he have forgotten. He did not want to alert her and he certainly did not want Suzy getting in the way as she seemed intent on doing so of late. When savouring thoughts of Melissa, Suzy always seemed to push her way into the forefront of his mind. Angrily he shook his head trying to dispel the image of Suzy and was frustrated as it was one that was becoming increasingly frequent. His agitation was gradually increasing and he fleetingly looked at his watch wondering why they had not arrived at a hotel yet. Glancing out of the window he noticed a more urban landscape and thought he could not be that far away now from a hotel. Taking a breath and trying to remain fixated on Melissa he closed his eyes and began murmuring her name under his breath while stroking his groin. Jerked out of his reverie by the sudden stop of the taxi outside the hotel. He got out of the taxi and brushed the driver off as he paid the fare and hastily grabbed his bags from the ground, turning on his heel walked through the revolving doors at the entrance to the Hotel Michael.

Once inside he gathered his thoughts and taking in his surroundings thought the hotel looked a little shabby as he approached the check in desk. Pasting a charming smile on his face he ran a hand through his hair while dropping his bag onto the floor and asked if they had a room available for one night. Luckily for him they had several rooms available and in his mind he was not that surprised given the decor and lack of visible staff. However, grudgingly he gave thanks to the taxi driver as it suited his needs and in the morning he would set off to Caberfeidh. Once in his room he showered and fell onto the bed closing his eyes just for a second and fell into a restless sleep. His dreams were one of torment and longing and unable to sleep he got out of bed and went into the bathroom to splash cold water on his face. Staring at himself in the mirror he grimaced then stretched his neck in a circular motion and rolled his shoulders. Gripped by a sudden rage he swiped at the shelf below the mirror smashing the ornamental glass dishes on to the floor. Restless, agitated and seemingly possessed he walked back into the bedroom and took out his maps from his bag. Scattering them over the bed he began checking and re-checking the route to

Caberfeidh and almost laughed aloud at the unexpected turn of events. He knew Melissa's parents were wealthy but he did not realise just how much that wealth amounted to. Even Melissa informed him that she was totally shocked to find out the extent of it. Why they had not told her about the other properties he could not fathom.

Caberfeidh... he breathed while lying back on the bed looking up at the ceiling. Repeating the name over and over to the empty space around him he did not notice the dark shadow in the room and fell back into a fitful sleep. Adam felt unusually energised and rested considering he remembered getting up through the night and after a shower he packed what little he had back into his bag and went down to check out without stopping for breakfast. At the desk he settled his bill and stepped outside into the cold dank morning air. Pulling his coat tighter around him he hailed a taxi and not long after was deposited outside the nearest car hire facility. Taking no more time than was necessary, impatient now to get going he completed the paperwork and grabbed the keys from the assistants hands. Without wasting anymore time flung his bag onto the back seat of the car and punched in the postcode of Caberfeidh.

Adam was oblivious to the dramatic landscape as he sped out of Edinburgh and headed towards the highlands but as each mile came and went he slowly began to take note. Upon reaching the same stretch of road that the Melissa and Suzy had traveled on only days ago he felt an almost magnetic pull of which he couldn't explain. There was hardly any other traffic on the road so he pulled over to the side and got out of the car. Suddenly, raised voices from behind him caused him to turn sharply but there was no-one there. Blinking rapidly he took in the scenery. Snow capped mountains surrounded him on both sides with a heavy mist that hung low in the sky. Looking around again he became more aware of the fine drizzle that was wetting his skin and closing his eyes he tilted his head towards the sky feeling somewhat cleansed. Opening his eyes abruptly he turned sharply once more as he was sure he felt someone push his shoulder. But that was nonsense. He was in the middle of the highlands, no other cars, no other people and nothing to see except the odd glimpse of mountain through the thick grey mist. This time he heard a whisper brush past his ear and he scratched it with his fingers while looking for anything, anything at all including a shadow.

His mind flashed back to when he was a child, the day that his parents had died. He remembered being there but it was though he was watching himself from a distance. He saw his mother crying on the floor of the cabin, screaming in terror, pointing at him and then at his father and he saw himself holding the knife. I know... she kept screaming...I know...it is him.....I can feel it....he is here...at his father .... It is true...it is true... her eyes shining with pain and knowledge and his father just laughed at her...cold... and unfeeling with a murderous intention in his wild eyes...His father paced the small cabin inside the boat shouting...Do it son...do it now...Adam did not hesitate...his mother's silence was deafening as the knife was plunged deep into her heart. Still laughing his father stood facing his son...it is true...it has come to pass ... power will be ours...and with that he dropped to his knees flinging his arms heavenwards in thanks and in that instant he saw the knife plunge into his own heart and the laughter died on his lips. Adam felt comforted by the dark mist that furled around him and he obeyed each command the voice gave him. He was still young and although part of him was trying to fight it, he was too weak, his body seemingly acted of its own accord. He felt nothing as he doused their bodies with petrol and threw the match that caused the explosion. That was the last time he saw his parents. The force of the explosion sent him up into the air and he landed in the dinghy only to be found less than an hour later. He could not speak and he would not move. It was weeks and months of therapy before Adam returned to the family home.

Adam shivered and shook himself free of the memories and getting back in the car he did not stop again until he reached the village where Caberfeidh stood.

CHAPTER TWENTY

Anna ushered Melissa and Suzy into the large house and in her excitement and longing momentarily forgot that Melissa must be overwhelmed and of course still grieving. After apologising and letting the girls go up to the bedrooms Anna sighed contentedly and remembered the day as though it was yesterday when Melissa's mother called her into the study and told her she was leaving to go to Caberfeidh. She sat in stunned silence not sure if she was being punished for something she did or did not do. Much to her relief it turned out that it was a promotion and one of which Melissa's mother was placing a lot of trust in her but also to her dismay it meant leaving the little girl she had come to love. Trying to politely refuse the post as she was happy working at Fairwinds and even happier caring for Melissa. Melissa's mother remained adamant brushing all of Anna's objections away and would hear no more on the matter. With a heavy heart Anna got up and closing the door gently behind her walked down the hallway and went through a side door and disappeared through the hedges into the walled garden to seek some solace. She needed to compose herself before facing the little girl she was so very fond of. As she sat quietly on a weather beaten bench she was not immune to the scent of jasmine and lavender which mingled in the air, which sought to comfort her.

Twisting her fingers in her lap she thought about what Caberfeidh would be like and would she find it easy to settle knowing that she would miss Melissa terribly. She had not been at Fairwinds as long as some of the other staff but it seemed long enough for Melissa's mother to trust her with running a household. She couldn't help but think it strange that Caberfeidh had never been mentioned, not to her knowledge, by Mrs Conway herself or indeed any of the other staff. Mulling it over she wasn't sure she even knew how to pronounce it correctly. Caber-Fay... she said aloud... Hmmm... That sounded right... She said with a smile and rolled the name 'Caberfeidh' around her tongue for good measure. She glanced over to the far end of the walled garden where a cherry blossom tree stood in an abundance of pink. Feeling a soft breeze caress her cheek she reached up to touch where it had warmed her skin and thinking she had just been kissed felt suddenly at ease and content. Caberfeidh... She said again to the breeze that gently whipped the leaves up around her feet. Closing her eyes and tilting her face towards the sky she nearly jumped out of her skin when she felt the softness that could only be fur brush up against her legs.

'Where have you come from? She asked as she bent to stroke the gleaming black fur of the resident Tomcat that would sometimes be seen in and around the estate. No one knew who it belonged to as it would appear for a day or two and then disappear for weeks even months. The cat replied by purring very loudly and rolling onto its back so that Anna could get better access to its belly. 'Well what do you think about what's just happened then? Anna asked the cat in a conversational manner. I wish I did not have to go... Anna whispered sadly... But I have not the choice.... Dear little Melissa... I will miss her something rotten.... She murmured while continuing to tickle the cats stomach. In answer the cat rolled back onto its legs and jumped up onto the space next to Anna on the bench and unceremoniously made itself comfortable on her knee. The breeze died down and Anna was grateful for the cats warmth. The cat looked up at Anna as it nudged her hand purring softly and while Anna continued to stroke the cat she was comforted with thoughts telling her it was going to be okay. One day she would see Melissa again. Making some tea in the vast kitchen Anna looked out of the window and over the rugged landscape that she had fallen in love with on sight. Stirring the sugar aimlessly she smiled as she noticed the big black tomcat chasing leaves in the garden and just as she noticed the cat, the cat looked back at Anna and she swore that it was the same cat, even though she knew that would be impossible.

Melissa and Suzy reached the upper floor and amidst the wonderment of fine tapestries that had been lovingly restored and which now hung high on the walls. They looked in all the rooms as they went not being able to decide which ones they were going to stay in. They passed small treasures of times gone past and of paintings that detailed beautiful, wild landscapes and Melissa couldn't help but stop every few minutes to look deeply into the paintings which she wanted to transport herself too. Suzy was effected deeply by some of the paintings but kept shaking her head and kept telling herself that she was being to whimsical. Melissa stepped into the fourth room she had came to and knew in an instant that this was the one for her. Suzy stood behind her peering over her shoulder and Melissa declared aloud that this was the one.

She followed Melissa into the room and joined her at the window as she studied what lay below.

"Breathtaking"... Melissa breathed... "Don't you think?" She asked Suzy as her heart quickened inside her chest. Below them both was a large garden adorned with a pond and statues at one end on one side and vegetable plots and a herb garden on the other. There was a colourful mixture of flowers and shrubs that bordered the lawn that sloped off until it met with a small stone wall that enclosed the garden below. Mid point along the wall they could see a gate which led out into an open area of gently sloping hills with grass the shade of emeralds. Mountains stood sentry in the distance giving the feeling of being enclosed by giants. A few tress dotted themselves at several intervals that led the way to a small copse. They could just make out what looked like a small bridge so wondered if there was a loch nearby. Closing her eyes Melissa followed the ground trodden path to the bridge using the trees to guide her. She heard the tinkle of water before she approached the bridge. Standing in the centre of the bridge she looked around as far as she could see and felt her body come alive and her heart began pounding excitedly. She followed the course of the small burn as it snaked its way alongside the trees and towards a rocky outcrop with a cairn next to it. She imagined what it would have been like to lift up her skirt and splashing the ground either side as she jumped into the burn. She ran in the burns path until she came upon the cairn and looked down as the water rushed off the edge, flowing rapidly over the rocks that jutted out from the small outcrop. Below where she stood the loch stretched across the glen and was calm and still with the reflection of the mountains gracing its surface.

Blinking rapidly she shut down the mental image as the girl she saw in her minds eye was the same girl who invaded her dreams. Rubbing her arms she turned and smiling at Suzy gestured that Suzy now find the room that she would feel comfortable staying in. Dragging her eyes away from the window Suzy was as transfixed as Melissa but for a very different reason. As out of the corner of her eye she had spotted a man wearing nothing but a pair of light coloured breeches with one foot up on the small stone wall who appeared to be staring out into the distance in the same way Melissa was. She could only assume that Melissa had missed him as she hadn't prodded Suzy in the ribs like she normally would in that teasing manner she always used. Suzy noticed even from this distance he was tall and broad with marks on his back and arms that she could not make out from where she stood but that she was sure were tattoos. His hair appeared quite light but not quite blonde but her eyes kept going back to his arms. His hair was long for a man as she could see a small ponytail that lay on the back of his neck. As he flexed his muscles she swallowed audibly and stood riveted unable to move. Getting sweaty palms she rubbed them on her jeans and squinted as she saw him remove his foot from the wall as he bent to pick up a bag of some sorts. Slinging it over his shoulder he glanced back at the house and looked up to the window where Melissa and Suzy stood. Suzy gasped and reached out to steady herself on the glass, glad that Melissa had moved away and was headed towards the door. He smiled up at her and she felt a white hot heat circulate throughout her body, twisting reluctantly away from the window as Melissa called her to go find a room, she swung her head back around towards the window but he was gone. Melissa oblivious to Suzy's discomfit and already half out of the door, Suzy had no choice but to follow Melissa back out into the hall and deciding on the room next to where Melissa was going to stay hugged herself and knew that coming to Scotland had been the right thing to do.

Much later they sat with Anna in the large kitchen laughing and talking while Anna told them of the years that she had spent at Caberfeidh and some of the stories about the staff that had come and gone over the years. Now there was just a handful of staff left who were almost like family to Anna. The two girls in turn brought Anna up to date on Melissa's life and of Suzy's antics. Anna sat and listened to the two girls chatter and felt so happy to see Melissa again she thought she might burst from it. She cried with them as the spoke about the death of Melissa parents and laughed with them while hearing tales of some of their exploits. Tired and content they both returned to their rooms and after a hug goodnight in the hall went into their own rooms. Unbeknown to each other they followed each others movements which led them to the window to stare out into the night.

At breakfast the next morning Suzy thought about the man she had seen the day before and it was on the tip of her tongue to ask Anna about him when there was a knock at the door. Wondering who that could be Anna looked at the two girls and asked if they were expecting anyone. When both girls looked at her blankly shrugging their shoulders, she got up to answer the door.

As Anna opened the door Adam stood on the porch tall and smug. Immediately Anna felt a shiver go down her neck and felt a deep distrust for this man.

"Hello Sir... May I help you?..

"Yes you may," Adam answered in a clipped tone. "I am here to see Melissa", and he put his foot out to stop Anna from closing the door which he had sensed she was just about to do. Realising her mistake she took a deep breath trying to shake off the alarm bells that were ringing in her head and looked at him matter-of-factly.

"I'm sorry sir but I'm afraid I don't know who you mean." Anna said shakily. Pushing her aside he strode into the hall and shouted out Melissa's name.

Suzy dropped her knife on the plate and it clattered to the floor upon disbelieving hearing what could only be Adam's voice. Bending down to retrieve the knife she was overcome with a nauseating feeling of panic. She watched in slow motion as Melissa jumped up out of the chair and laughing excitedly she exited the kitchen running out into the hall to greet Adam. Running into Adams arms Melissa was giddy with happiness as he swung her up and around in his arms. Putting her down gently he tucked her hair behind her ear and kissed her lightly upon her cheek.

"I cannot believe it is really you!" Melissa exclaimed. "How did you ever find me here?" and dragging him into the kitchen she did not notice Anna's sheer look of terror. Dancing into the kitchen with Adam close behind her she began to busy herself about the kitchen, not even waiting for Anna to come back, she sat Adam down at the table and with a flourish poured some tea and popped some bread into the toaster.

"I take it you must be hungry?" She asked smiling and not quite believing that Adam was sitting here in this kitchen with her and Suzy.

"I'm famished," Adam replied laughing at Melissa's exuberance and rubbed his stomach in mock pretence of being starving.

Suzy got up from the table and trying not to look daggers at Adam as she passed him, made her excuses saying she thought they might like a few moments alone. Adam sat watching Suzy and could feel her fear feed his ego and could not prevent savouring the sweet taste of victory within his grasp. Smiling at Melissa he momentarily forgot what he was here to do as he relaxed into the domestic bliss that Melissa was creating. Once out of the kitchen Suzy looked about for Anna who had not come in to the kitchen with Adam and Melissa and who seemed to have disappeared. Leaning up against the wall trying to steady her breaths that were on the brink of becoming a panic attack she quickly tried to think of a way to get Adam to leave. But knowing it was going to be an almost impossible task now that he was here wanted to cry at the sheer frustration of it.

Unaware of Suzy's worry and of Anna's sudden disappearance Melissa contented herself with making Adam breakfast and telling him about the journey up here and holding his hands tightly she told him how happy she was to see him. Outside pacing the garden Anna cursed under her breath for she recognised Adam Donnell and in the years she had spent at Caberfeidh had learnt a thing or two which had tested her resolve and love for Melissa. Just beyond the gates to the long drive which led to the door of Caberfeidh two men sat in a dark car partially hidden by the trees.

"Well boss... He's here."

"Yes... so I see" Winchester remarked with a smirk.

CHAPTER TWENTY-ONE

Suzy gasped and swallowed audibly with a frisson of shock, as she looked up to find the tall commanding figure of Kian standing over her. So lost in thoughts of Adam and Melissa and what she could do to try and keep them apart she was unaware that her initial search for Anna had led her to where she now sat with her head in her hands. As Kian stood over Suzy he couldn't help but stand just a little taller when he caught the expression of female appreciation in her eyes and remembered the way she had been staring at him from the window. He narrowed his own eyes as he saw how quickly she covered her expression up.

"You must be Suzy?" Kian asked abruptly in a commanding Scottish accent .

He tried not to smile at the way her eyes widened when he called her by name. Suzy feeling just a tad nervous and having no idea how he knew her name quickly shut her mouth before answering with one her usual quips. Trying to stretch her neck so that she could attempt to see around his hulking great form felt like she was some sort of insect as he didn't move but remained intent on scrutinising her. She felt sure that in the stillness enveloping them she could hear each breath he took and starting to feel panicked but not threatened tried to look directly up at him.

As he stood staring down at Suzy he probed gently with his mind but could sense nothing, he was sure...no in fact he was certain....but then why was there nothing? Half squinting Suzy began to feel a little braver and slowly opened both her eyes to guage his expression and paused when she noticed a glazed look on his face. She was struck by three things while openly appraising him without him seeming to notice. He was much taller than she thought he was, he had to be over six foot and at least three foot across the shoulders. He has the most hypnotic Scottish accent she had ever heard and he seemed like the worst kind of womaniser she had ever had the good fortune to be this close too. The tattoos rippled and seduced the onlooker as he involuntary flexed his muscles and Suzy began to rub her now damp palms down the denim of her jeans and couldn't stop the thoughts that came crashing into her head at 90 miles an hour. ...His lightly golden tanned body was naked as he leant over her while she was in a state of undress....her breathes heavy ...his hands gripping her hair...

"Suzy?" Kian asked, this time not needing to use any power to know that he had had the desired effect.

Blushing from her toes to her roots Suzy, feeling flustered, embarrassed and like she was an insect that had now just been burnt by the sun through a magnifying glass, nearly fell back down as she tried to get up from under his sexually emanating scrutiny. He probed once more and not only was he confused but the fact he could still sense nothing except a void made him take a step back wondering what tricks twas a foot. Suzy finally gathered herself together and stood up to face him. Finding the courage to look directly into his eyes, she was sure she could feel something but it seemed to hover just beyond her comprehension. She automatically reached out to place her hand on his chest and was shocked at how quickly Kian had moved to grab her wrist before she made contact.

"What are you doing lass?" he said with a slight edge to his voice. Suzy shrinking back from him began to utter incomprehensible words and finally spluttered a reply.

"I could ask you the very same question?" She stated as he let go of her wrist. Proud of herself she placed her hands on her hips and stood facing him squarely with a confidence she didn't quite feel.

"Do you ken who ye are lass?"

"Of course I know who I am!" Suzy's eyes widened along with her stance as she bit out her reply and Kian took a step back seeing the fire in her eyes while secretly admiring her grit. Holding his hands up and palms out in mock surrender he hid his smile as Suzy's eyes widened even more at the size of his hands. Several naughty thoughts were competing against each other inside her head for example, where he grabs her behind with those hands... as well as... the one where he he uses those hands to slowly stroke her thighs, teasing her gently... Shutting her eyes to shut out the thoughts while counting to three she then opened them while jutting her chin out and glaringly asked in the most la-di-da accent she could muster.

"Just how do you know my name anyhow?" while shrinking back slightly at sounding so childish even to her own ears.

For an instant Kian stood absolutely stock still before leaning backwards and in the first time in more years he cared to count let out a roar of laughter that Suzy swore made the ground shake beneath her feet. As Suzy stood there feeling a little mortified at sounding childish and blushing embarrassingly due to the many sexual thoughts that wouldn't leave her minds eye, felt miserable and wanted nothing more than the ground to open up and swallow her right there and then.

Be careful what you wish for lass...Suzy heard the whispered words in her mind and looked sharply up at Kian while at the same time Kian took a step closer to Suzy so that she could feel his warm breath on her face. Gripping her shoulders tightly was an involuntary reflex as the realisation she had heard his thoughts fought for a place at the front of his mind.

Did ye hear me lass?...Can you feel it?....Kian whispered once more questioningly and desperately wishing that he had made some kind of break-through. Suzy could do nothing but stare wide eyed and open mouthed up a Kian while her brain tried to work out just what was happening here. She tried to shrug her shoulders but the grip Kian had on them rooted her to the spot while the most languid feeling of hot molten lead seemed to be snaking its way from his fingers into her skin, making her feel slightly queasy. Kian felt the familiar feelings of nausea and abruptly let go of Suzy. A need to protect Suzy hummed through his veins and he managed to just stop himself in time from reaching out to draw her close until the nausea passed and he mentally shook his head as he remembered that same feeling. Shutting down the uncomfortable memories before they took hold and assailed his body he put his hand in his pocket and touched the peace stone that he had carried with him all these years. Closing his eyes briefly he concentrated on clearing his own mind while probing Suzy's mind once more to make sure he hadn't imagined it.

Although Suzy still could not move, the hot leaden pressure she had felt as Kian gripped her shoulders started to dissipate along with the nausea the instant contact was broken. Noticing subtle changes in Kian's expression Suzy was fascinated how each change happened in slow motion.

The more she stared at Kian's face the more she began to hear her own heart beat thudding in her chest. As each beat grew louder she felt transported to a place untouched by time. Squinting her eyes shut she tried to capture and absorb every wave of peace and love enveloping her and desperately wanted to memorise this feeling of intense warmth that was nothing like she had ever felt before. She saw herself in her minds eye turn towards a whisper while trying to locate the person it was coming from. As the voice was becoming clearer she could see Kian calling her towards him. Why is that oaf calling me....he is standing right in front of me? As Suzy screwed her eyes closed and began to fall to the ground Kian naturally reached for Suzy and caught her before she hit the ground.

Kian carried Suzy back to his room at the great house which was tucked away towards the back of the great house and overlooked the vast rugged landscape that looked harsh this time of year but to Kian looked beautiful no matter the season. Suzy weighed no more than a feather he thought as he gently laid her down on his bed. Fearing she would wake at any moment and scream profanities at him and dimly conscious of his fingers still burning after the feel of her skin had gone. He stood back and watched her sleeping form. He could not understand why he could not sense her. His knowledge of who he was and what he was had always driven him to this point but in all the years he had watched from a distance expecting to see his twin or to at least feel their presence in his mind there had been nothing....still there was nothing... he shook his head and started to breath slowly and deeply whilst looking down at Suzy and opened his mind and his soul.

Suzy stared wide eyed at her surroundings and began to pinch herself to make sure she wasn't dreaming. It was like something out of one of those fantasy films she loved to watch, curled up on her tatty sink-into sofa wearing her favourite fluffy PJ's. All around her was lush green meadows filled with wildflowers giving vibrant bursts of colour as far as she could see. She could hear water bubbling away in the background and as she turned her head to see a stream started to form before her eyes. Thinking that it wouldn't be complete without a waterfall, one appeared from a crop of rocks that also appeared and as her mind filled with thoughts of the sun warming her face and blue skies with small wispy clouds she looked up to see exactly what she was imagining. Jogging up and down on the spot a giggle erupted from her and just as abruptly stopped when dark thoughts began to scatter across her mind turning the blue sky dark and stormy. Squeezing her eyes shut she counted to ten and repeated to her herself over and over to stop being fanciful and that she was obviously having the weirdest dream ever as her brain was frazzled with all that had gone on. Opening her eyes and expecting to still be sat under the tree deep in thought she jumped when she was still stood in the same place surrounded by scenes that played out in her head. Frowning slightly she tried to concentrate and wake herself up but after several attempts of closing her eyes, clicking her heels the same as Dorothy did in the wizard of Oz and thinking if it worked for Dorothy then maybe it would work for her but still finding herself stood in the same place staring at the most amazing, colourful landscape she began to panic.

Helpless to intervene Kian watched Suzy's smiling dreamily expression turn in to one of panic and fear. He wondered silently if she was starting to experience the same nauseating violent lurches that he had experienced when he felt her eyes bore into the back of him the day she stood watching him from her window. He knew she just had to remain focused and let the feelings wash over her but he was still perplexed as to how they had never crossed paths before. He remembered how sick he felt and had avoided her the last day or so just watching her from afar but she had showed no signs of what he had experienced until now. He desperately wanted to reach down and stroke her face to try and ease the pain that was becoming more and more visible on her face.

Bile rose in Suzy's throat and she tried to fight back the waves of nausea that seemed to grip her. The fantastical landscape that had surrounded her just a moment ago had shifted into one that was cold, desolate and vast of which seemed to be closing in on her causing her to feel suffocated and scared so she couldn't move. Swallowing the bile back she tried to reach out into the cold dark void but could feel and see nothing. Fear and panic were threatening to overwhelm her and she turned her head side to side, squeezing her eyes shut and opening them desperately looking and searching for a way to shut the images off in her head and return to the calm, beautiful surroundings and to the last image she remembered of sitting under the oak tree. She abruptly fell to her knees and gripped her head as the splinter of voices and images collided with one another in a white hot heat of pain and suffering mixed with passion, warmth and love. A furious storm of emotions fought violently vying for recognition but so fearful of what was happening to her and of her mind shutting down at the continued onslaught and violent waves of nausea she opened her mouth to scream and then just as suddenly as it started, it stopped and she heard a voice that grew louder the more she focused in on it.

"Suzy...lass you are going to be ok... just focus...focus on my voice..." Unable to stand and watch her suffer any longer Kian reached down and gently touched her face unsure what consequences that might have. Pulling his thoughts back from any unequivocal damage that he may have just caused he stroked her cheek noting just how soft her skin was and how warm it was under his touch. Seeing the colour coming back into her cheeks he swore under his breath and snatched his hand away just as she opened her eyes and looked directly up at him whilst a tear slid down the same cheek that just a moment ago he had forbiddingly caressed.

"Kian?" ...Suzy questioned horsely... "What is going on?...

"Och lass I wish it be a simple thing I need to tell ye...But here... let me get you something to eat and drink to settle that stomach of yours and I will try to help ye by answering ye questions." Suzy nodded dumbly and watch Kian leave the room and quickly shot up once she realised she was in fact not in her own room but lying in his bed. Too fraught to do anything else and a thousand images and questions dancing around in her head she collapsed back down in his bed and too fearful of closing her eyes just stared blankly up at the canopy above her head. Suddenly remembering the reasons she had wondered out in to the grounds and had sat beneath the tree she went to jump out of the huge bed just as Kian entered the room carrying a delicious smelling croissant and a hot chocolate....no time to wonder how he knew they were her favourites she greedily grabbed the croissant and began to stuff it in her mouth as though she hadn't eaten for a week. Realising Kian was watching her every move she stopped self consciously as he gently placed the hot chocolate in her out-stretched hand and then he walked to the chair by the window and sat down before facing her again. She nearly spat the hot chocolate out when she heard his voice in her head and her eyes shot up to meet his.

She wasn't sure how much more time had passed but she didn't move while she sat there opened mouthed listening to Kian tell her the biggest load of nonsense she had ever heard. She could hear his voice loud in the room echoing around the walls and she couldn't now shake off the realisation that she could also hear him inside her head like a gentle hand offering comfort and protection. Kian eventually rose up from the chair and slowly walked to the window keeping his back to her. He willed her to just trust in him but knew that what he had just told her would most likely have someone else running for the telephone to call for the police. As he stared solemnly out at the rough beauty of this sometimes desolate lonely place he remembered all the years he had watched and waited but never truly knowing or believing until the moment he had made a connection with Suzy and prayed in the old language he was right.

"Kian...?" her voice was soft...barely a whisper...and he closed his eyes clenching his fist around the tapestry that he still insisted hung at the window. "Can you hear me...? Does it work...? Can you tell me what you have just told me once again..? Her voice was tentative tinged with curiosity and as

Kian turned to face her with his eyes still closed she heard his answer in her mind and felt the electricity crackling between them as he opened his eyes slowly staring deep into her soul.

CHAPTER TWENTY-TWO

It had been a long time since he had felt the need to seek the power of the Runes but he had begun to feel the subtle shifts of change. Now that Melissa was here and he had told Suzy what she was and what they needed to do he knew that it would get stronger until everyone was where they should be. Casting the stones he let his hands hover over them and in an ancient tongue started to speak words that had not left his tongue for decades. Slipping under its power he closed his eyes and let himself sink back to see if he could have done anything differently.

...Kinnon followed Ciar into the night and knew instantly where he was headed as he had seen Maura head in this very same direction not moments ago. He knew Ciar was taking a risk but unable to deter, or for that matter want to, he just did his duty and made sure he came to no harm.

Night had fallen on the village and not too far away there stood a forrest which led down to the loch. It was a magical place, she thought, so peaceful and hidden from prying eyes and smiled as the pale moonlight touched the waters surface so that each gentle ripple could be caught and savoured as though wanting to capture this moment. Time stood still and it was as though heaven itself had intervened she thought as she stood by the edge of the loch. The silence was deafening and each breath she took she feared would wake the dead. Slowly she reached for her clothing and started to gently strip it away from her body. As she removed each item she felt the soft breeze on her skin and remembered his touch. Caressing her skin she imagined it was his fingers not her own that slowly made a trail down her face and tilted her face up towards the moons light. With a feather light touch her fingers made a trail down her throat and across her collarbone. Breathing slowly but steadily she let her fingers trail further between her breasts as though marking her heart only for him. Shivering not with the cold but with anticipation she knew it was only moments before she gave herself to him . Looking up towards the moon she prayed he would still be able to make it. How was it possible she thought... he was powerful, handsome, a warrior and the Laird's son...

Placing her foot gingerly into the cool water of the loch she tensed just for a second as the impact of the cold made her shudder. Taking a deep breath she glided into the water until she was waist deep. Unaware she was being watched she tilted her head back and floated upon the water's surface bathed in the moon's light and the smile of heaven. The water lapped seductively all around her and never had she felt so at peace despite the unrest in the village. Determined not to think of war and what that would mean she turned on to her front and began taking long gracefully strokes through the water.

He crouched low in the surrounding trees. He felt a slight unease at not alerting her to his presence but she was so beautiful in this unguarded moment he could do nothing but just watch her. Such intense feeling's were so alien to him that he only recognised them for being a rare and precious thing and could nay thank the gods that he had been chosen to feel such a wondrous thing. He knew war with the MacDonnell's was threatening the future of his clan and she was in the centre of it but just watching her float on the waters surface bathed in moonlight in this secret place they shared he did not have the heart to break the spell. She moved through the water with such ease and grace he found it hard to match it to the girl he new on land who was spirited, alone and stubborn. Smiling to himself he decided he had waited long enough. Like the hunter he was he reached the bank of the loch with making a sound and the silence was like a blanket that surrounded them both in this moment. Seeing the pile of clothes she had left and briefly looking out to where she was to make sure she hadn't heard or spotted him he reached for the garment that lay on top. Taking it in his hands he brought it to his face and inhaled her scent as though it was for the last time.

Filling his lungs deeply and without making a sound he stripped naked and entered the loch making his way to her silently and stealthily. She stopped for a second, treading water, and looked towards the bank where she had left her clothes not able to see or sense any danger.

She was just about to head back when she was dragged under water. Fighting for air she kicked and tried to scream until he released her and when they broke the surface she flung her head back. He half lifted her out of the loch as he caught her in his strong powerful arms before she could escape. The spray from her hair landed on the water's surface like bubbles . She didn't know whether to hit him over the head or kiss him. Heat seared her skin despite the water's coldness where his hands held her tightly. Looking down into his face she felt such an overriding rush of passion she felt like she had sinned right in the centre of the loch. Easing her body down against his own he did not take his eyes from her face. He was once again caught by the strange stormy depths of her olive green eyes. Taking her mouth in his own he possessed her with everything he had. Hands and lips fought over each other in a bid to out do each other. Breathing hard and fast while still treading water he ran his hands over her hair and down her back while at the same time pulling her into him. She felt glorious in his embrace and knew no words were needed as he took possession of her mouth and of her body.

Leading her back towards the edge of the loch he vowed that he would never let any harm come to her. Lifting her out of the water he carried her up to where their clothes lay in a haphazard pile. Laying her down gently on the moss he knelt beside her.

"Ye ken I'd ne'er let any harm come to ye lass?"

"Och get away wi yr'self I ken that..." she replied while planting small kisses all over his face although in her heart and mind she knew he could never openly claim her and it was only a matter of time before he broke her heart. She concealed her thoughts from him by looking away but she couldn't stop a lone tear that snaked its way down her face. Catching it with his fingers he wiped it away with a heavy heart. Turning her head to face him he kissed her. Burning passion fuelled his kisses as he sought to show her just how much he truly loved her. Not wanting to give herself up so easily she tried to push him away but he held fast to her lips and her body.

She could not stop the onslaught of emotions that battled within her and held on to him tightly as his kisses sought to ease her. Pictures of them as children flashed before her and his staunch declaration on protecting her still resonated within her as well as all the times he had been there for her. Lying against the soft earth she gave herself up to him as his lips and hands sought to touch, possess and command her body. She could not deny the emotional rage threatening to engulf her and returned his kisses and caresses with as much vigour as his own. Forcing her hands above her head he pinned her down while he ravished her neck and worked his way down her throat and to her breasts. There he gloried and sucked leisurely taking one nipple in his mouth at a time and playing with it with his tongue, teasing and tormenting her. Unable to do anything but lay under him while he tormented her she sighed contentedly while her breaths came quicker and shallower.

Each touch of his lips was like an electric frisson, overpowering and dominating. As he placed his lips on her skin he felt an overpowering need to conquer and possess. She could not bear the wait as it was excruciating and tormented her very core. His need drove him to punish her, mark her and tease her until she surrendered completely. Breaking contact he lifted himself from her body and stared deep into her eyes. Looking into his stormy depths she felt her heart splinter as she was sure she could see tiny fissions of doubt. As he stared into her green pools of liquid his love and passion spilled into every fibre of his being. He would never let her go, she was his, forever. Slowly he trailed kisses down her body and she lay there helpless to his sweet torment the moonlight lighting the way. As the feel of his lips sliding down her body sealed her fate she loosened one of her hands and ran her fingers lightly down his back. The feather light touch of her fingers fuelled his need to kiss and own every part of her skin. Her fingers began to dig deeper into his skin and as they did so it prompted him lower and lower. He reached the centre of her core and an animal instinct took over. Arching her back widely she felt the brutal lashings of his mouth and tongue against her very being and as she thrashed against the onslaught he pinned her down with a subtle strength only meant for her to enjoy. She exploded in a starburst of light and fireworks and trembled helplessly. Filled with a roaring, primitive feeling of triumph he crawled back up her body kissing each part of her exposed skin and delighted in the tiny tremors she responded with. Catching her mouth in his own he kissed her commandingly while she gave herself up and kissed him back feverishly. Reluctantly rolling off her body and onto the mossy floor next to her he reached for her hand and held it gently. They both lay there in their secret place surrounded by woodland and listened to the sound of the nearby waterfall joining the water next to them. Lost in their own thoughts he knew not how long he could go before taking her completely. She already know she could belong to no other.

In the distance he could hear his name being shouted echoing through the forest until it reached the lovers and he gripped her hand more tightly.

" Tis time my bonnie wee lass," he whispered as she turned to face him on the ground and was unable to stop a tear from escaping. Wiping it way gently with his free hand he swallowed hard and reached in to kiss her with such longing and meaning it scattered her emotions to the wind.

"Do ye hae to go?" she asked softly.

"Ye ken I have tae go before they'd be finding us..." and reluctantly he let go of her hand and getting up from the ground he didn't take his eyes off her while he dressed.

Helping her up he picked up her simple dress and slipped it over her head, caressing her body as he pulled the dress into place. The shouts were getting louder and kissing her goodbye he left knowing it would only be a matter of time before war broke out between the clans but he could not stop how he felt about her.

She stood alone by the loch and after straightening her dress she bent to scoop up the cool water of the loch and splash her face which she was sure would give her away. Even though she was an outcast she still worried about what the villagers might think. Gingerly making her way back towards the croft she stopped and turned back from where she had laid with Ciar and sighed deeply for she knew that he would never give himself to her completely and she had to remain strong accepting that this was the most he would be able to offer her.

A wise old owl hooted into the night sky as it watched the scene unfold below and it took flight from the branch just before it saw a dark mist gather at the place where the lovers lay. A branch snapped under the weight of his foot and Kinnon looked around to make sure that both Maura and Ciar were out of earshot and on their way back towards the village. Spying the dark mist he crouched down and did not breath. Watching the dark mist weave itself in and around the place where he knew they had laid he was fascinated by the power of the dark king but knew at all costs he had to protect Ciar. He knew Maura had a watcher but in all the years he had watched Ciar grow and turn into the fine man he was, he had never seen or felt Maura's watcher and did not know whether that was normal or not. He knew it would not be long before battle would ensue he only hoped that Ciar had the good sense to stop doing the right thing and take Maura completely to free their souls then his job would be completed...

Kian placed the Runes back in the soft cloth and took steadying breaths as he loosened the spell that he'd surrounded himself in and that had been their home for many years. He looked at the clock. He knew that Conrad had experienced visions and he hoped that Melissa had started to as well. He reflected on what he had remembered and the one thing that stood out was that he had never able to see or feel Suzy's presence. Used to the tricks played by the dark master he did not know whether she could be trusted despite what they had shared. The creators had been known to meddle when they should not have. Changing the paths of destiny of those who were watched or putting obstacles in the way to help or to hinder. Was Suzy a help or a hinderance? He wondered.

CHAPTER TWENTY-THREE

The Mistress of light sat alone gently running her fingertips over the surface of the glistening pool at her feet. How many times had she done precisely the same thing over the millennia and nothing had changed. This time it felt different, she was not sure why or how but instinctively she felt the subtle shifts like grains of sand falling through the deep chasms of time. Knowing she was alone and would not be disturbed, for there was no one to disturb her, she took the human form on once more and with a gentle caress of the air around her summoned up images that she had kept hidden away. Many of them were of people, places and events that she had observed, sometimes openly and unbeknown to them and to her own kind. None before her had been so fascinated about the human complexities as she had been and continued to be, despite knowing what a dangerous game she played. It was true that some had peered through the veils of time to watch their creations come together, but only a few had meddled as the penalty was too great and was something she witnessed every century when she stepped into the stones and saw the soulless eyes stare back, empty, cold and dark, despite previously filled with light, love and warmth. Some of the images that danced around her were forbidden. Her race was considered amongst their own as above reproach and unparalleled. Emotions were beneath them and all the nuances they brought. She whispered on the breeze for one of the images to come forward so that she could study it in greater detail. Oh they knew all there was to know about human fragilities and how they interacted when experiencing great emotion, but none were permitted to experience it for themselves despite the ability to change form, sift through time and become one of them if that was what they desired. She turned the image up and over and around whilst studying every feature, every element every sound and touch. She closed her human eyes and reached out to touch the scene in front of her.

The spray from her hair landed on the water's surface like bubbles . She didn't know whether to hit him over the head or kiss him. Heat seared her skin despite the water's coldness where his hands held her tightly. Looking down into his face she felt such an overriding rush of passion she felt like she had sinned right in the centre of the loch. Easing her body down against his own he did not take his eyes from her face. He was once again caught by the strange stormy depths of her olive green eyes. Taking her mouth in his own he possessed her with everything he had. Hands and lips fought over each other in a bid to out do each other. Breathing hard and fast while still treading water he ran his hands over her hair and down her back while at the same time pulling her into him. She felt glorious in his embrace and knew no words were needed as he took possession of her mouth and of her body.

As her finger penetrated the scene she had brought forth it dispersed into a thousand fragments and she went back to peering into the glistening pool. As the unbidden thought of touch refused to leave her mind she pondered silently if she could give up her existence and experience the raw passion and emotion that the last two she had created shared. She felt their uniqueness at their birth and had risked all to become part of their world in one lifetime and then the next. Never before had she felt such a strong need to bear witness first hand to what she created and now she was consumed with knowledge that was dangerous and forbidden.

He shifted between mist and form... undecided which suited him better in his current mood. As mist his essence snaked across the vast empty space that he occupied in a place only one other knew existed. He could appear as fine and as delicate as morning dew or at the same speed as a single thought he could became a dark, freezing, furling fog that trapped all that he surrounded. Shifting into his usual glamour of what some may mistake as Fey he summoned the looking glass and watched as it hovered ever so slightly beyond his glamours reach. Many times he had summoned the glass to watch the game in play but never once had he felt the compulsion to look at her. Filled with a sudden rage he cursed the looking glass into a thousand shards but it remained tauntingly beyond his grasp, beyond his words and more frustratingly beyond his power. His reflection stared back at him while the space he overwhelmed crackled with dark energy. An achingly, haunting eerie spine chilling roar escaped his lips as he tried to erase the image the looking glass presented to him. It could never be...It was time to show his hand.

Conrad sat and wiped at his brow to remove a glisten of sweat as he let himself into his office. Feeling absurdly like he was trespassing as it was the early hours of the morning he paused at the entrance to the vault taking a moment to breathe normally. After waking disheveled and the note still crumpled in his hand and somewhat convinced that he was somehow living in a movie he knew nothing about and without any thought as to what he looked like jumped into his car and sped over to his offices to convince himself that whatever answers teased the periphery of his mind lay just beyond that door. He looked down at the crumpled note and almost lovingly flattened it out. As his fingers smoothed the parchment it was written on, the words came alive and began to glow whilst changing form. The door to the vault swung open and Conrad too stunned, stepped forward into the vault as though for the first time.

As each step took him deeper into the vault, he became highly attuned to the electrical pulses around him. It was as though he could slow every passing thought and dwell on it for an eternity. Dissecting it and analysing it from every perspective, touch it and feel it in a way that he had never thought possible. His heartbeat became the only sound he could hear and its steadying beat drove him forward and further to find answers. Memories crashed and collided vying for attention like waves in a storm crashing against hard unmovable rocks . The deeper he ventured into the vault he was only dimly aware that doors appeared and opened where before he could have sworn there had been none. The rational part of his mind was trying but failing to control the irrational part as he couldn't deny what he was seeing and feeling. He reached out to try and brush the objects he passed as their memories called to him, pulling him into their depths but his feet drove him further into the darkness, instinct being his only guide and his heartbeat being the only sound. As he stepped through each door the objects he passed became older but more familiar to him and the urge to touch, linger and feel its energy became almost overwhelming. From deep within him he felt the presence of Ciar stir and he took the letter out of his pocket to feel the words slide under his fingertips alive with their meaning.

His heartbeat that had been strong and steady, driving him forward deeper and deeper into the vault, began to slow and his breath was becoming visible with each exhale. It was certainly colder now than when he first entered but he had yet to feel a chill on his skin. Consciously touching his arm he was almost seared from the heat he was radiating. Feeling a subtle shift in the energy around him he stopped and tried to let his eyes adjust to the dim light. He stood in awe at what he could only describe as like being trapped in some surreal reality show as he slowly surveyed what lay before him . Fine furniture had been neatly stacked up against the crumbling brick wall. How had he never known of the vaults depth...Had his father known? Chests of jewels and art were piled up on the opposite side along with large tombs and scrolls still protected by their leather cases. Why had the compulsion to keep going which had driven him this far into the vault suddenly left him... His eyes caught a glimpse of a high backed chair and the hairs on his arms stood erect despite radiating searing heat. Slowly crossing the width of the passage to reach it he instantly recognised the ornate carvings and the image of Melissa and the elegant drawing room at fairwinds flashed before his eyes.

Och now...she hasna changed one wee bit....Conrad jerked at the sound of his own voice but that wasn't his own voice...What the fuck was going on...he thought and gripped the back of the chair and at the same time he wished for an electric light switch to turn on so he could give some semblance of sanity to this insane situation. As soon as the thought came and went the place where he stood was lit up with beacons of fire on the walls, evenly spread apart and on both sides. Breathing slowly but steadily he turned in a slow circle and in that minute felt that this was some evil trick. As he looked both at the direction he was facing and back to the direction he had come from he could see nothing but an empty back space, no path, no walls, no lights...no objects....nothing. All the fires went out, bile started to rise in his throat and he bent over unable to prevent the bile from leaving his body. The only thing he felt as he reached blindly out was the chair and as his grip touched the ornate carvings he was transported to the room where the chair had sat regally behind the table he remembered from Melissa's study.

Conrad was crouched in a corner of what looked like a large stone built room and in front of him he saw the desk and the chair that only a fraction of a second ago had been in his grip. Two men seemed to be arguing behind the desk and a third man who stood off to one side kept looking over to where Conrad crouched and squinted his eyes. Conrad didn't dare breath or move and did not even try to assimilate what he was seeing or for that matter what his logical mind was telling him where he was and who was stood in front of him. His own heartbeat had slowed so much so that Conrad thought this was to be his final resting place but the voices of the men in the room seemed to be getting louder and Conrad tried to concentrate on what they were saying. As the first rays of dawn lit the room one of the men who had been arguing banged his fist down on the desk and his words reverberated around the room.

"I dinna care wha' ye say...Maura and me will be wed with or without ye blessing. As soon as I've slain the MacDonells I will be back to claim her as my own."

Conrad could hear the barely controlled anger in that voice and couldn't help admire what could only be bravado as the man he said it too was much larger.

"You'll NAE be wedded to THAT lass... As ye FATHER and as ye LAIRD...mi word is FINAL." The chair fell backwards as the bigger of the two men flung his arms wide open. While despite being smaller the other man was still a giant and he squared his shoulders about to offer a retort and then abruptly turned on his heel and in that instant that mans eyes met Conrad's and Conrad saw his own eyes staring back.

As he left the room Conrad's breaths came swiftly and his heartbeat pounded deafeningly within his chest and just before he closed his eyes wishing that somehow all of this would just go away he heard the larger man say to the man who had been standing in the corner in a cold emotionless tone.

"Ye must dispose of the lass afore Ciar returns. I'll nae hae hir ruin mi sons life like her mother ruined mi life long friend's...NOW GOAED...

Kinnon silently nodded his acquiescence and after being dismissed he looked directly over to where Conrad now stood, his eyes probing and once locked they fiercely bored into Conrad's own. Instead of crumpling to the floor when the man had finally broken the hold he blinked and found himself back in the hidden depths of the vault still with his hand gripped tightly on the back of the chair. Wanting to get out of there as fast as he could and find Melissa to convince himself that all he was experiencing wasn't some sign of insanity his foot kicked over a pouch full of stones.

Bending down to retrieve them Conrad head exploded with flashbacks of Maura and Ciar and of each stones significance. Breathing hard and finally trusting in his instincts he blindly ran through the vault hoping it was the way out and never having felt so conflicted, knew he must get to Melissa before it was too late.

That's it Conrad....follow your instinct...let your heartbeat guide you to the truth and the answers you seek.... With a contented sigh she rose from the glistening pool.

CHAPTER TWENTY-FOUR

Suzy wandered out of her room to go and find Melissa, still in a complete daze and not quite believing what Kian had just told her, despite repeating it to her several times. As she walked along the landing she was certain that she could hear the voices from each portrait as she passed. Quickening her pace she cornered the top of the stairs and was tempted to see if anything she had learned about herself had released any Mary Poppins style abilities and had a sudden urge to slide down the bannister. Just as she was about to burst into song and jump up onto the bannister she spied Adam below.

Instantly she snapped her mouth closed and scrambled backwards so that she was pressed firmly with her back to the wall in the hope he wouldn't spy her standing there. If anything Kian had told her found a way into her rational mind and actually stayed there it was that she should always trust in her instincts, and her instincts about Adam made her feel like she had a demon clawing its way out of her stomach. She dared to take a small step forward, to glance down and see which direction Adam had taken. When she leaned forward to get a better look Adams eyes slammed into hers and she turned so fast she tripped over her own feet and fell flat on her face. Breathing hard she clambered clumsily to get up, not really having any idea what or why she had instinctively wanted to flee. Shaking her head and telling herself that she was well and truly losing her marbles she stood up straight and breathed in deeply, smiling stupidly to herself just as her world went black and she slumped into his waiting arms.

Breathing hard and fast he caught her swiftly and silently sometimes wondering where his speed and strength came from. Picking her up he carried her down the stairs checking there was no one else around. Walking blatantly out of the front entrance and unceremoniously dumping Suzy into the back of his car, he glanced briefly around and back at the house. He then got in to the car and smiling sinisterly he turned the key in the ignition and put his foot forcefully down on the accelerator causing the gravel to fly as he skidded away from Caberfeidh.

Kian dropped the fork he had been holding in his hand and turned swiftly to look back at Caberfeidh, the screech of tyres caused all his muscles to tense as the noise to him was like a thousand claws dancing on a blackboard. He began to run back towards the house berating himself for venturing this far away. He was so close to crossing the line with Suzy, he had to escape her and in doing so fled to the sanctuary of this small garden he had created a long time ago and that had lay hidden from human eyes for an equal amount of years. Running as fast as the wind he himself screeched to a halt at the spot there the car had left its tyre marks in the gravel.

Opening his mind he tried to pinpoint the direction the car had gone once it had left the driveway and had headed out on the main road. Trying desperately to locate Suzy's scent and her soul he felt a dark blanket block his every probe. Breathing steadily he shut his eyes and tried once more... In his mind he saw her face as she had laid there on his bed, her eyes closed and her lips tinged with the human blood that ran through her veins. His own blood began to pound within his body and arching his back he let the unbidden feelings wash over him. Sudden emptiness invaded and covered him like a second skin and he could feel its icy cold loneliness steep into ever cell of his human form snapping him back to an upright position with eyes steely grey and glazed over like a feral animal about to kill.

It was impossible... he thought.... They had connected....or so he thought? It was truly her... he was so sure of it. This should never had happened....As he stood motionless digging his heels further into the gravel and letting his thoughts and feelings surface he was suddenly surprised to find that through the several layers of his mind, he heard the faint sound of Melissa's voice calling out. Like some kind of switch he mentally shut them down and turned facing the direction of her voice and masking his true feelings he easily slid the look of nonchalance across his features. Melissa approached him slightly breathlessly.

"Did you hear that awful noise? Melissa asked bending down slightly hands on knees while catching her breath. "I was expecting to find some beast of a sports car sat here the way its tyres screeched and I ran to greet whoever it might be."

"Och well... It not be someone arriving but someone leaving..." Kian remained cautious as he didn't want to give any cause for concern when they may be none but his insides were screaming that Suzy didn't get into the car by herself and drive off.

"Have you seen Suzy by any chance? I haven't seen her since breakfast? I lost track of time as I finally found Anna in the library and ending up getting lost in some rare books that I had discovered." Melissa straightened up and looked at

Kian expectantly. Not given to lying but clever at only alluding to the truth he replied in his usual calm hypnotic tone.

"I spoke with Suzy not that long ago and I was in fact in the kitchen just making a drink to take to her when I heard the same...how did you put it...och now.....'that awful noise'..." As Kian finished to pause for breath he raised one of his eyebrows at Melissa who wasn't fooled for one minute. She had caught the way Suzy had dribbled over Kian and he hadn't realised that Melissa had seen. If she didn't know Suzy any better she would hazard a guess that Suzy has used all her feminine wiles to bag Kian while she had been holed up in the library too engrossed in what she had found and was probably draped over her bed waiting for Kian to find her and some sort of semi naked undress! Kian was just too much of a gentleman it would seem. Smiling radiantly at Kian and feeling a little embarrassed she winked knowingly and pivoted away and practically skipped up the steps to the entrance. Kian just stood there a little dumbstruck as he detected subtle waves of romantic notions radiating from Melissa. Opening his eyes wider as he watched her skip away from him, he couldn't possibly be imagining that Melissa was contemplating anything untoward between himself and Suzy! Dear god... he thought... dismissing the idea before it had time to form. He cursed as the unbidden knowledge of what it felt like to touch her skin that had been so soft under his fingers filtered through his defence.

As Melissa disappeared through the door Kian looked back towards the road and with his mind probed further than he had ever dared before in this lifetime. He mentally winced as his mind hit the equivalent of a steel wall. Thick and impenetrable an invisible sheet of darkness the likes of Kian have never thought possible blocked him and pushed his magic back as easily as though squatting a fly. His breath came hard and fast as his thoughts raced, tumbled and fought for order. Pulling himself in he slowly gripped the one stone he had always carried with him and caressed it's smooth surface seeking guidance. He felt nothing....masking the torrent of emotions that simmered beneath his cool features he strode back towards the house and without giving the bewildered looking Anna his normal cursory nod and hello as he passed her in the hall he headed straight for his room. Pushing the door wide open he stepped over the threshold and knew before his foot had brushed the floor that she was gone. How could he have been so blind...so wrong. His last conscious thought was that...It could not be... then everything went still and his world went black as his body shook violently and he doubled over in unimaginable pain.

Adam looked over to where Suzy's drugged and hapless form lay sprawled over the back seat of the car. He wasn't sure how far he had driven and shaking his head he wasn't entirely sure how he had found this place and was now staring down at her prone body. Knowing that Suzy wouldn't regain consciousness for a few hours yet he got out of the car and straightened his back while stretching his arms outwards almost embracing the landscape before him. Just a few feet away was a moss and heather bitten cairn that at first glance could have easily been mistaken for just a haphazard pile of rocks. A hundred or so yards behind the cairn stood an old bothy that looked as though it had stood empty for several years. With a purposeful stride Adam strolled past the cairn and went inside the bothy. Once inside Adam had to duck so that he didn't hit his head on the low ceilings and screwed his nose up in disgust at the foul stench that instantly clung to him as he stepped further inside.

The bothy was made up of three empty rooms, all of which which had bare stone walls and a single source of water made up of a tap protruding from the wall . To enter one of the rooms, he had to climb three steps and once there he noticed an open disused fire and wooden bench that he wasn't entirely sure would be safe to sit on. Perfect, he thought as he retraced his steps back towards the car. Once there he unceremoniously pulled Suzy from the car and dragged her limp body inside the bothy to the room that had the disused fireplace. Propping her up against the bench he left her there on the cold stone floor and went back out to the car to get the rope from the boot that he had noticed earlier. Not once had he stopped to see if anyone had followed him and neither had he given any thought to anyone that might be watching him. He was driven by instinct and a need that consumed him so deeply that he would laugh hysterically, should anyone try to even guess what thoughts ran amok through his mind. Methodically and silently he returned to where he had dumped Suzy's body and began in earnest to secure her to the bench, then testing to see if it could be moved. He snickered when he realised that the bench was actually bolted into the stone floor with a steel chain that had been hidden by a crumbling cloth. Looking up sharply as he sensed a subtle shift in Suzy's breathing he then relaxed as it was obvious to him that it would be some time indeed before she would open her eyes. He only wished he could be here to witness it.

Smiling to himself he busily secured Suzy's hands behind her back and tightly fastened the rope to the bench and then made sure that her feet were bound together to prevent her from moving. For a fleeting second he thought to find some kindling to start a fire but after looking at his watch and out of the small open window, he noticed darkness was fast approaching and thought better of it. Taking a lingering look at Suzy he turned his back and left her there in the empty, cold, stone room with no heat, food or means to access the inviting single tap that protruded from the wall opposite should she ever regain consciousness . Robotically Adam got back in to his car and started the engine, pausing only for a second before speeding away from the disused bothy with the mysteriously covered cairn, marking its place in the forebodding rugged landscape.

"I don't think he knows we are here boss" Mr Winchesters lackey commented.

"Take him out at the next corner but keep the lights off." The instruction was clear, succinct and punctuated with a sadistic tone that brooked no argument. As their car neared the tail lights of the car in front the lackey swore as Adam slammed on the brakes so hard it left him no choice but to slam his own brakes on and swerve to avoid ploughing into the back of Adam's car. It was precisely what Adam wanted and when his car had screeched to a halt he effortlessly removed his seatbelt and before stepping out of his car, pulled the glove compartment open to take out a small handgun. As though in a trance he didn't question how Mr Winchester had come to be there or how a gun was in the glove compartment. It was eerily silent but unaware he casually walked over to the other car which had rolled onto its roof and as Adam bent to check the inhabitants he pointed the gun and snarled at the blood stained face of Mr Winchester. Glancing briefly at the lackey and only dimly registering that he wasn't breathing, he glanced back at Mr Winchester who was frantically battling with the seat belt but was unable to free himself. Without hesitation Adam aimed the gun at Mr Winchesters head and with a smile he told Mr Winchester the debt was now paid. A dark mist surrounded Adam as he returned to his car and started the engine. Putting the car into reverse he backed up but before driving off he flooded the narrow road ahead with the cars headlamps and looked across to the car that Mr Winchester had been in.

The mist thickened and moved lovingly, almost caressing the scene that lay before Adam, swallowing it and containing it. In the minutes that passed Adam watched, as the whole scene was engulfed until there was nothing but darkness. Putting the car into drive he put his foot down and raced back to Caberfeidh. The only face he now saw was Melissa's.

CHAPTER TWENTY-FIVE

Conrad was not sure how he had made it out of the vault tonight without wanting to check straight in to a hospital to get psychiatric help. All he could think about was Melissa and the presence of something bigger and beyond his imaginings that compelled his every step, his every breath and his every action. Pacing around his apartment he began tossing things into a bag while talking into his mobile that was balanced precariously under his chin. Feeling his impatience rising with every minute that passed, his mobile phone slipped from its resting place tucked under his chin and it fell to the floor without him noticing as he grabbed his keys. He switched off the lights only to switch them back on while stepping over all the things he had thrown on the floor in his haste to pack to pick his phone back up and taking one last sweep of the apartment satisfied that he had everything he needed, let the door click softly shut behind him.

As he ran down the steps two at a time to get to the lower ground floor that housed all the residents cars, he thought it could easily be mistaken for a car show room given the amount of high performance cars lined up in neat rows. Upon hearing the mono tone sound of his car unlocking he raised the boot and threw his holdall in and nearly knocked himself out as he went to close it at the same time as reaching in to grab his mobile from the side pocket of his bag. Finally he sat in the car and put the smaller backpack on the passenger seat. He then took a deep breath and started the engine which purred into life belying the power that vibrated under his fingertips and like a beast ready to pounce the car just waited for a feather light touch on the accelerator, so that it could unleash its supremacy and leave the prison of the car park. Conrad smoothly slipped the car into gear and slowly exited the car park and switching the display to his iPod library he browsed his playlists until he found the one he wanted and knew that the sweet beats of trance would mirror his emotions on the journey ahead.

As the city lights faded and the darkness of the open road enveloped him he put his foot down and the engine needing no encouragement, came to life and like any beast it left its mark where the tyres scorched the road. Conrad relaxed back into the seat and felt a now familiar stirring inside and heard the faint echo of Ciar's impatient voice telling him to hurry. Looking over to the passenger seat he reached out and rummaged in the small backpack until his hand gripped the small pouch he had taken from the vault. As he turned the pouch over in his hand he felt the stones inside tumble and touch beneath his fingertips and a comforting warmth spread through his fingers and up his arm until his whole body seemed to come alive. Never taking his eyes from the road he reluctantly let go of the pouch and concentrated on the road signs as he sped past them. He knew when he had crossed the border as Ciar's stirrings and mutterings became more pronounced and Conrad becoming so attuned to the whispers, began to have difficulty trying to decipher Ciar's words. As the sun rose in the sky Conrad's vista was taken up with different hues of orange and red that glistened over the top of the greenest hills he had ever seen. Having had Ciar's ramblings in his head for the last seven hours as well as the time Conrad had spent in the service station grabbing a much needed coffee it took him a few moments to realise that he no longer heard Ciar's deep impatient voice rambling on in his ear. Easing off the accelerator he pulled over to the side of the road and got out of the car to stretch his legs. He looked at his watch and knew he was only a couple of hours away and in his haste to get here he hadn't actually thought about what he was going to say to Melissa. He did know that if he was her he wouldn't take much notice of some guy who hadn't slept, probably smelt a bit too and had driven hundreds of miles to tell her that he kept having the weirdest dreams and could hear voices in his head. He almost laughed out loud as this was the first time in his structured and orderly life that he had no plan. In all the years he had been practicing law he had been meticulous over detail and at possibly the most important moment in his life he didn't have a plan.

Closing his eyes and tilting his face up to the first rays of daylight he felt free. For the first time in a long time his mind and his body felt free. As well as opening his eyes he opened up his senses and gave in to them. The sky's colours took on a new vividness as the oranges sparkled against the clearest blue.

"Och mi wee laddie... ye ken this is home....tis a beautiful sight." Conrad couldn't disagree as he heard Ciar's voice strong and clear in his head. As Conrad's eyes roamed the landscape he was struck by just how strongly he felt a sense of belonging. He absorbed every detail from how many shades of green the grass was on the hills to how vibrant the purple heather was dotted randomly on the hillside. A gentle breeze teased the hair on the back of his neck and he tilted his head back once more in surrender leaving his face exposed to the suns morning rays. Breathing deeply his nostrils filled with air that carried the whispers of past battles and he sighed heavily as though bearing witness to the many scenes of devastation. Opening his eyes he looked all around him and not another soul was to be seen on the empty road that stretched out before him that snaked its way between the glorious hills and a crystalline clear loch. He had heard as a boy that the air was different in Scotland and while he stood here in this moment breathing deeply the history of these rich lands he truly understood what they meant. Getting back into his car he sat for a moment reluctant to leave the spot that had afforded him a true measure of peace and certainty but feeling the rumblings of Ciar within, he started up the engine and almost in anticipation of his foot pressing down on the accelerator the car roared into life and took off.

Glancing at the SatNav he saw that the turning should just be ahead on the left. Conrad slowed the car down and pulled into the side of the road. Gripping the steering wheel he suddenly realised just how absurd this situation was and could not quite believe that he had driven here about to tell Melissa some mad cap story. Would she laugh at him?...Would she even agree to see him?... Jesus... he thought... he hadn't even notified her that he was just about to appear at her door. Running his fingers through his hair he suddenly banged his fist down on the wheel and looked sharply up at his reflection in the rearview mirror.

His eyes were no longer the colour of a stormy grey winter eve. The eyes that looked back at him where steely ice blue with flecks of molten silver. He raised his fingers to his face and traced the stubble that had appeared in just the last few hours and he could unexpectedly feel his hair brush the back his neck where as before he could only feel the gentle caress of a breeze. He looked down at his shirt and noticed that the buttons were beginning to come lose as the cloth strained against his skin and that his trousers now felt uncomfortable and constrictive around his thighs. He looked down at the soft covering of hair on his broad forearms and could swear they appeared darker. He was changing. He could feel it even if he couldn't explain it. It was impossible he thought...or was it? He looked agin at his reflection and it was him but not him.

"Och mi we laddie it be happ'n... just like she foretold..." Ciar's commanding, strong and bold voice was as clear as the hand Conrad held up in front of his face. This had never been a factor in any of the strange mutterings he had put up with in his head. Nor was it something that had even seemed possible. Not from his visions. Not from his experience in the vault.

"You are not me." Conrad stated calmly and with an equally commanding tone.

"Och laddie...whisht yer mind...I ken I'm nae ye. Yer generation are far too wee..." Ciar teased as Conrad looked back down at his shirt and trousers and saw they were no longer straining or constricting. "It felt good thou' aye? Tae be a big, brawny lad? With a soft chuckle Ciar's voice faded and

Conrad stared at his reflection once more. Hmmm... he thought... the stubble was still there along with his hair that brushed his collar and the more he stared at the eyes that stared right back the more solid he felt and sure that destiny was called destiny for a reason.

A whaling police siren put an end to Conrad's contemplative misgivings and the reasons that had compelled him to act so uncharacteristically and he watched as several cars went speeding past heading in the opposite direction. Something big must have happened, he thought to himself as he had encountered so few cars on the journey here to have the peace disrupted by several police cars seemed out of place somehow. His lawyers head wanted to follow the police cars but he could feel Ciar's growing impatience and restlessness inside of him and intuitively he felt that perhaps that wouldn't be the only time he saw a police car today. As abruptly as the sirens pierced the silence their tuneless sound became a distant echo and when there was only silence once more, did Conrad start the engine and slowly drive the few hundred yards to the entrance of Caberfeidh.

As he turned off the road into the drive he passed under a stone archway that stretched between two large pillars with the name Caberfeidh engraved into the each slab. Atop of each pillar a lifelike antlered stags head sat prominently staring down at who so ever should pass beneath its hawk like stare. Following the driveway he drove through a wooded area and felt his heart begin to pound as the house came into view. If a house could be described as regal yet beautiful, large but not vast, fairytale in nature yet the scene of battles and bloodshed and seeming ancient yet modern at the same time it was Caberfeidh. So many different contradictory thoughts and emotions flooded his mind as he sat speechless staring at the house. It was all he had imagined it would be and more that first day he had learnt of Melissa's inheritance. It felt familiar somehow and not just from the memorandum detailing its particulars and whereabouts. He sat tapping the steering wheel trying to remember where from as it continued to nag at him. Knowing as soon as he stopped thinking about it he would remember he drove the remaining short distance to the main house.

Stepping out of the car he half expected the huge front door of the house to be flung open and for Melissa to come running down the steps with arms open wide smiling and laughing as though greeting a lover. Giving himself a mental shake he tugged at an imaginary suit jacket which was his usual attire as he walked around to the boot to grab his bag. Clicking the boot open he remembered that he had given little thought to what he had put on in his haste to get here. He looked down at a faded grey T-shirt haphazardly tucked in to the front of a black pair of jeans that fit snugly to his well portioned muscular thighs despite the earlier unwelcome interference from Ciar. He smiled to himself knowing that he certainly didn't need any interference from Ciar as he shook his legs slightly to loosen the jeans from around his bulge. Glad he had at least put on a well polished pair of ted bakers he ran his hand once more through his thick slightly wavy dark hair which was only just beginning to show the tiniest amount of grey at his temples and again felt the soft stubble that had sprouted up on his face in the last few hours. Oh well, he though there was nothing he could do about that now and finally grabbing his bag from out of the boot pushed it down for it to click gently and silently back in to place and turned to face Caberfeidh and taking a deep breath he walked towards the door. As he reached out to ring the rather ornate ironclad bell to announce his arrival the door opened wide and Conrad took a step back almost falling off the top step as he took in the man standing before him.

Conrad had always been proud of his low maintenance, naturally gifted 6'2 foot frame with wide shoulders, broad arms, slim waist, tight buttocks and muscular thighs but was momentarily taken aback by the man standing opposite staring down at him quizzically. The man stood a good several inches taller than Conrad and for that matter seemed to be a good few inches bigger all round. He was about to introduce himself and ask to see Melissa when the mans quizzical glare suddenly broke into an infectious smile and giving Conrad no time to react grabbed Conrad and pulled him in to a bear hug, Conrad had no choice but to submit to the bigger mans strength and a little disturbed by the mans actions cleared his throat as he gently disengaged from the huge arms that seemed reluctant to let go. He stepped back safely this time and held his hand out expectantly and in a voice sounding calm to his own ears looked at the man who still stood there with a beaming face.

"I'm Conrad Mckenzie and you are?"

"Och I ken who ye are Conrad McKenzie." Kian replied jovially, slightly bemused at the range of emotions that flickered across Conrad's face. "Ye better come in ."

Conrad was nonplussed as he was led in to the house and as soon as he stepped over the threshold his mind exploded and dropping to his knees he grabbed his head to stop it from splitting in two. Och here we go again....and was briefly reminded of Suzy but unable to dwell on her whereabouts he immediately bent down to help Conrad up from his knees and supported his weight easily, despite Conrad's purely male physique and led him up the stairs and into his room where he had lain Suzy down on his bed in what seemed like only hours ago. Making Conrad comfortable on the bed Kian left him and went back down to fetch Conrad's bag and to get a few provisions he knew he would be needing from the kitchen. As he made his way down the hall he spied Anna sitting in the library looking feverish as she sat behind a pile of books, unnoticed he carried on until he reached the kitchen and raided the cupboards grabbing what he needed and then his eyes whipped round to the kitchen door that led out into the garden as he heard it swing open with a crash and saw Adam enter looking a little dishevelled. With a grunt in acknowledgement and his senses preoccupied with the man upstairs he hesitated just for a moment as though waiting for something to come to him but instead he turned his back on Adam and strode purposefully back down the hall and up the stairs to where Conrad lay thrashing about in the bed, shirt in tatters on the floor beside the bed. As Kian watched helpless to intervene he put the provisions down on the table and sat down in the same chair from where he had watched Suzy thrash about in his bed and now he watched Conrad go through the same pain and pleasure that the knowledge would bring, he could only hope that that when Conrad came through it he didn't up and run like Suzy had seemed to have done.

Settling back in his chair and closing his eyes he could only see Suzy's delicate features a breath away from his lips. Despite opening his eyes to stop the images from tormenting him, her face would not leave him. For a short time he transported himself back to the night he watched Maura and Ciar make love next to the loch and even knowing that as a watcher it was forbidden to feel that one emotion for another he had always believed himself incapable. Now he wondered... Listening to Conrad grunt and groan he knew better to interfere and could only pray it would be over by morning as he was determined to track Suzy down to wherever she had taken off to but was loath to leave Conrad as it was his duty to watch over him. It niggled him that she could have just taken off if indeed thats what she had done. He knew that the hire car Melissa and Suzy had travelled up in had been collected so that only left Adams car. His mind flashed back to Adams dishevelled appearance in the kitchen and Kian cursed. He had been so taken up with Melissa's arrival and then of Suzy there had been no time to use his power to learn more about Adam and in doing so he couldn't help but now think he had missed something vital. Torn between his need to stay with Conrad and find answers to Suzy's whereabouts his thoughts kept returning to Adam. Closing his eyes he reached out with his senses to locate Adam. Shifting his body weight in his chair he reached out and probed wider. Nothing.

Conrad screamed aloud and thrashed wildly in the bed with the pain of the memories that were now filling his mind causing Kian to pull back all of his senses and refocus on the man on his bed. Tormented by Suzy, torn between his duty to stay with Conrad and an instinctive impulse to find Adam, for the first time in his existence Kian cursed the very reason for his being and remained where he sat not taking his eyes from Conrad knowing he was unable to seek Adam out until after the compulsion to stay at Conrad's side had finally freed him.

CHAPTER TWENTY-SIX

Anna sat in the library after spending the day avoiding everyone in the house by busying herself in the kitchen and making herself scarce in the herb gardens. She caught a glimpse of Kian as he walked past the doorway and noted how purposeful he looked. She had a feeling in the pit of her stomach that was not unlike the one she had that day she was told to leave and take up her post here. She couldn't help but wonder if it was two coincidental that Melissa should turn up here after so long and then Adam. There was something about Adam she couldn't quite put her finger on but there was something amiss and she had felt it the instant she had answered the door to him. She worried for Melissa but was unsure why. Even Kian who had been with her for several years now seemed to be keeping a distance which was unusual for him, not that she had much opportunity to speak to him over the last couple of days. The time she had spent with Melissa earlier in the library had filled her day with so much happiness it almost made up for all the lost years she had missed watching Melissa growing up. Just seeing Melissa's face light up when she exclaimed over this book then that book until an unruly pile of several books sat on the large oak table in the centre of the library. Melissa was so enraptured by their contents chatted none stop while Anna could do nothing except hug herself, smiling and nodding in reply, happy and contented just to see her after all this time. Although she sat there now and kept touching the books one by one whilst muttering to herself. Unable to shake the feeling in the pit of her stomach she eventually rose from the chair and noticing the time made her way quietly out of the library switching the lights off as she went. Tomorrow morning she decided, she would keep a closer eye on Melissa and get to know Suzy a little better as she could tell that both Melissa and Suzy were very close, perhaps Suzy could go some way to putting her mind at ease regarding her misgivings.

Anna awoke the next morning after a fitful sleep and decided that today she would spend some more time with Melissa and Suzy and find out as much as she could about Adam. Although the house was its usual quiet self at this time in the morning, Anna made her way along the corridor and down the sweeping staircase sensing something different about the house and every now and again Anna stopped in her tracks unsure what is was that was making her feel so on edge. When she reached the kitchen she put the kettle on and sat down at the table looking up at the clock. She supposed it was still early for the girls as it had only just gone 6am but Kian was normally an early riser and she had always trusted his judgement, maybe she could ask him to watch Adam and see if he sensed something a bit off about the man. In the past he had always had a canny knack of knowing things or saying just the right thing to cheer her up on one of her melancholy days. she had half expected him to be sat here already filling his face with her home made bread and jam. She could almost swear that Kian must have heard her as he appeared in the kitchen just a few moments later.

"Morning tae ye Anna." Kian spoke quietly and not in his usual jovial good humoured morning voice as he made his way directly to the sink to get a glass of water. Anna watched him as he stood in front of the sink and decided to get up from the chair and busy herself getting bowls, plates and an assortment of cutlery out to place on the table. She stayed focused on what she was doing when she replied.

"Morning Kian...Could I possibly speak to you about something that has been playing on my mind? "

"Aye ye ken ye can Anna, what ails ye?" Kian tensed slightly wondering if Anna somehow knew that he had another male in his room and was jumping to all sorts of conclusions. They both started to speak at the same time..

"I can explain...."

"I need to talk to you about that man Adam..." As Anna worriedly asked Kian about Adam, Kian sensed straight away that Anna was deeply troubled and at the same time relieved that she seemed to be unaware there was yet another visitor in the house and that he didn't have to explain Conrad's reason for being here just yet. However at the mention of Adam's name his mind flashed back to the way Adam had entered the kitchen the night before looking dishevelled and a little off. With his mind so pre-occupied with Conrad he hadn't stopped to question Adam and up until that point had had no reason to watch him more closely. If truth be told, before Conrad turned up, he was pre-occupied with Suzy and hadn't given much thought to Adam. He stood in the kitchen itching to get back to his room before Conrad should wake and trying to control his increasing anxiety to know if Suzy had returned he only half listened to what Anna was saying to him.

"...So if you wouldn't mind?...Kian?...Kian?" Anna repeated a little louder.

"Och sorry Anna...wudna mind what?" Kian, a little surprised at himself that he could have switched off so completely, smiled down at Anna while masking his own worries knowing what a devastating affect his smile would have and in response to Kian's beaming smile Anna shook her head at him muttering something about him being a typical male. Having no time to dissuade Anna of that notion he now concentrated on her words while she repeated her request to keep an eye on Adam and to see what he could glean from the man and his intentions while he was here. As Anna finished repeating her request and made herself busy again preparing some dough, Kian immediately felt relief that he could check on Conrad and promised Anna that he would keep a careful eye on Adam and would let her know of anything untoward that he might learn.

Carrying the glass of water back to his room a thousand questions ran through is mind. He automatically stopped outside of the door to Suzy's room and leant unconsciously towards the door to breath in her scent. The faint aroma of Dior teased his nostrils and he closed his eyes briefly breathing so deeply that her scent might penetrate his very being. Opening his mind he reached out through the door expecting to feel her and so that he could feel happier in the knowledge that she had returned. Nothing...not even the sound of gentle breathing. Just as he was about to place his hand on the door to open it, his own door opened and Conrad stood there half naked running his hand through his hair and rubbing his chin with bright feverish eyes that zoomed straight in on Kian, almost making him feel guilty for what he was about to do.

"What has happened to me?" Conrad asked without preamble. Kian snatched his hand away from Suzy's door as though burnt and straightening to his full height ushered Conrad back in to his room, masking his expression of wanting while clicking the door shut softly behind him. Conrad had gone to stand by the window with his back to Kian and waited for Kian to answer his question taking not so relaxing deep breaths. Despite knowing this day would eventually come Kian was at a slight loss on how to explain things to Conrad now the man was standing in this very room in front of his very eyes. After witnessing Conrad through this lifetime and previous lifetimes he had never really stopped to wonder what would actually happen after the soul he had been born to watch and protect should finally find its mate. Despite knowing that was the reason for his very existence he had never thought beyond his role and what it would mean. He had read teachings that described a watchers existence and all the responsibilities that came with it but there was nothing written that described the after event. What would happen to him, he wondered....what would happen to Suzy? He felt a deep darkening sinking feeling in the pit of his stomach and did not want to examine the feeling too closely afraid of where it might lead. Turning his attention back towards the man stood at his window Kian reached into his pocket and palmed the smooth surface of the stone he had carried around with him for centuries letting its power soothe his mind.

"I think ye should sit" When Kian spoke his voice was thick with emotion and despite the turbulence that thickened the air around him, his calm authoritative manor penetrated Conrad's spinning thoughts and Conrad sat without hesitation on the chair that Kian had occupied the night Suzy lay thrashing about in his bed. Pushing thoughts of Suzy away his stare locked with Conrad's and walking forward he closed the gap between them. As Conrad's expression changed from curiosity to fear at Kian's expression he went to stand but Kian reached him before he could move and as Kian placed his open palm on Conrad's shoulder to keep him in the chair Conrad instinctively shut his eyes bracing himself for some sort of pain. What Conrad actually felt, was all the feelings, thoughts and actions that several lifetimes had accumulated pour themselves into him. Pictures of people and places flashed one after another faster and faster almost making him dizzy. Unable to speak he sat utterly helpless as the images assaulted his mind and the thoughts and feelings of his past lives fought for space and recognition of their importance. As each image was replaced by a new one Conrad noted small changes like buildings becoming more modern, places becoming more recognisable and faces more familiar. All but one face changed and that was of Melissa's. Her face had not changed in the thousand images of her and them together that passed before him. The images told their own story and he knew without any doubts everything he had done had led him to finding Melissa. This moment was was like the unveiling of the creation of love and all the components that usually remained hidden from sight. Conrad felt the pressure of Kian's hand lighten on his shoulder and without blinking he looked into eyes that had held the knowledge of his existence for so long.

Recognising a subtle shift in Conrad Kian slowly removed his hand from Conrad's shoulder and took a step back. Shutting his eyes briefly he relaxed his body and took a deep breath preparing himself for the barrage of questions that Conrad would have. The seconds ticked by and the silence remained, just the slow steady beat of Conrad's heart could be heard in Kian's ear. Daring to open his eyes he waited and still with his back to Conrad spoke softly.

"Are ye not going tae say anything?"

Conrad sat and watched Kian's back, noting the small movements as he breathed in and out. He knew that he could not even begin to form the words that were stuck in his throat as it would be admitting to himself that beyond science there was magic. Beyond logic there was mystery. Beyond loving there was something so rare and precious that mere mortals wrote and dream't about it, yet some never finding it, yet here, right before his eyes Conrad had been shown the story of how souls were created. Of secrets that were only shown to those whose souls found each other. He was part of some bigger picture and had true meaning. Instead of the knowledge acting like a weight of burden, the knowledge felt light, it felt peaceful and harmonious, almost impossible to describe except to say it was like a kaleidoscope of colours that sparkled and shimmered with vivid hues. They exploded and blinded the observer and then like a wave rose high above the observer and then crashed magnificently down yet without harming. Turning into feather light speckles of every colour imaginable that bathed the onlooker in love, yearning and need for its mate. Warmth spread through Conrad as the realisation took a logical hold in his brain, all the dreams he had had, all the restless nights, the sparks that flew as he touched Melissa that very first time began to make some sort of sense now. That was why he was here. The urgency he had felt in having to get here to see her to tell her what had been happening to him was because he was truly meant to be with her. It was too much... too much and he fought momentarily in his mind for other reasons, other answers but as every fibre of his being burned with the new sensation of knowledge he had to admit that this was true, so very true and that it was something that just was.

The tension in Kian left him at the exact same moment that Conrad truly acknowledged what he was and who he was. As he turned to face Conrad in the chair he noticed a different aura that surrounded him, it was the one that used to surround Ciar. Smiling slowly he held out his hand.

"Ye are back"

"He is here, I feel him stronger than the others but it is me now. In this time it is me Conrad." Conrad's voice was strong and true and not for one minute did Kian doubt it. However Kian also knew that Ciar had played a bigger part in all of this than he cared to admit. Opening up his senses he just wanted to check and let out a deep soulful laugh as Ciar's words rang in his ear...Donna ye be thinking that I not be he're and see that ye be getting it right this time!...

Not quite sure why Kian had suddenly burst into laughter Conrad grunted and finally removing himself from the chair stood tall and stretched his arms above his head and clasping his right hand with his left swung his two arms behind his head making his chest swell. Kian did nothing but raise an eyebrow and walking to the wardrobe he pulled out one of his shirts and tossed it at Conrad telling him to make himself look decent as he was now going to have to explain Conrad's presence to Anna, dear sweet Anna, what she would make of things yet to pass Kian did not know. Hastily Conrad covered his torso up with the shirt Kian had flung at him and went into the bathroom that led off from the room to splash water over his face. He ran out of the bathroom and both men made for the door leading out to the hallway as they heard the raised voices from below.

CHAPTER TWENTY-SEVEN

He held her without touch and she felt his grip tighten around her neck while his aura surround her. No matter that he was her equal in every way they had been destined to always be opposites. He had no need to squeeze any tighter for her image would break into a thousand fragments. Disgusted with himself he made the image of her within his grip to one of her standing in human form and imagined her taking a brush and slowly running it through each strand of sparkling golden hair that graced the perfectly formed human head. Waving his hand through the image he summoned grey stones one on top of the other until all he saw was a wall of hard stone, grey, unyielding, bleak and everlasting.

His existence was a lonely one. Oh he relished pain, death and misfortune but if truth be known he was lonely. In over a millennia he had never felt what the humans referred to as loneliness. He could summon anything and everything whether he wished it or not, so great was his power. Except her power was just as great and after playing this game for so long they were now at an even score. Unusually for him, if indeed he could refer to himself as a him, he had to give her credit for lasting much longer than the others. He had never been replaced before and up until now he had never questioned it. Could he even be replaced... he wondered in this huge vast emptiness that he existed in. Sifting between human form and dark cold mist he circled the images he summoned of her and sneered at each form she took. Perhaps it was the frustration of knowing the score was equal that was now causing this unrest within him. He was fully aware of what emotions were and how they felt but he had never before felt inferior enough to experience any of them. He knew of her tricks and loathe to admit it he often used the same tricks to peer into the human realm and watch unbidden the story of each creation unfold. Except that she remained unaware and thats something he had preferred to stay the same. Sometimes he got as much sadistic enjoyment in knowing he was watching her meddle while meddling himself and for her to remain completely oblivious to it or to have even suspected it.

This time though he had meddled too often and the consequences of which were now just beginning to transpire. He thought gleefully back to the time he possessed Adam as a child and made him murder his own parents. The evil that ran through Adams veins was in fact him but it had all been so easy. On the very day of the last creation after the child's tinkling cry filtered through the realms to where she had stood in that pathetic circle of hers he knew then that if he could make her think that he would win this time and that she had been too late in saving that soul then he would have the advantage. Like a harp string that had been plucked it was her fearful reaction to that small possibility that had set his course of action. He had secretly watched her and her meddling without her knowledge and now when he was so close to victory and seeing her be replaced he felt what the humans called lonely. As the anger built and flooded through the molecules that made up this present form he felt a sense of rage that he could not define. Why should it matter of she was replaced. It had never mattered before whenever any of her predecessors had lost and then to be chained to their mark, only allowed to bear witness to a creation once in every hundred years.

She was different. He had felt it in that fleeting moment when she shielded the fear from her eyes and had stood her ground while he had wrapped his essence around her, whispering in her ear that the game had just begun.

He once again brought that final image of her to where he materialised into human form and just like he had watched countless human males through the centuries, he circled her.

Looking at her from every conceivable angle. He flung his arm out and made a section of the wall he had built earlier appear and imagined her hanging, limply, held to the wall by chains while blood ran down the crease of her breasts. Using one of his newly formed fingers he wiped a droplet of blood from her navel and brought it to his lips, tasting the essence of her being while he hovered in front of her. Swiping at the image he then summoned her upon a human bed with a sheet wrapped around one of her legs which left a leg exposed and draped carelessly over the edge. He had never partaken in what the humans called sex but he had witnessed a thousand times thinking it dirty and unnecessary. Except now he reached out to stroke her leg and as his hand went higher he found himself pulling back the sheets to look at the body she possessed.

Bitter and enraged he let out a piercing roar of anger and built a iron fortress around himself, only for him to morph into mist once more and snake his way through the iron bars that he had created. He had spent centuries in this vast empty space without once experiencing any kind of what you could call emotion to now experiencing a raft of different emotions. It was all her fault, he swore she would not win, he was too close and he summoned his looking glass. The only tangible item that connected the realms and caressing its smooth reflective surface he entered the glass to be taken to the human realm.

She felt the pull before she realised what it was. Changing from her usual form into her ethereal one she fought against the rising fear that began to engulf her. With all her power she willed her mind to be at peace and detach itself from feeling so she could fathom out what was going on. All she could ascertain was a need and a yearning so strong it shocked her. Despite being covered up in bitterness and loathing she felt it as clear as she felt all things. Surprise flooded her and for a moment she stopped time so that she could put things into perspective. Her first fear was that it was one of her souls was so conflicted and torn between love and fantasy that they did not believe. So unnaturally strange were the feelings taking over she had difficulty in finding its meaning. Even for the doubters there had always come a point when realisation hit them and they knew they were meant to be and any small flutter of emotion she felt had always blossomed. She felt confusion for the very first time as the more she probed this strange occurrence the more she realised it was something that she had never experienced before. Gone was the peace that normally surrounded her and in its place was fear and loathing that she couldn't shake. Heedless of the danger it could put her in she opened herself up more to the strange sensations that were taking over and at the moment she summoned her glistening pool to take her to the human realm she realised her error.

CHAPTER TWENTY-EIGHT

Sitting in the same spot at the table was Anna, just where Kian had left her what seemed a lifetime ago. Adam was there too looking like he had not yet cleaned himself from the night before. Also in the kitchen stood two police officers, one of which watched Conrad and Kian closely as both men entered the kitchen at the same time. Conrad's eyes went straight to Adam's and Adam's eyes spat sheer malice in Conrad's direction. Anna felt a little bewildered at the sight of yet another man whom she did not know, appearing in her home. She looked at all three men who made her kitchen feel like a small cave and shrank back into her seat instinctively preparing for an outbreak of male testosterone to explode.

Inspector Johnson was not a short man. He was in fact tall, some might say thin rather than athletic and had a weatherbeaten complexion from days spent out on the loch fishing, which these days he tended to do more of than actual police work in this part of the Highlands. This morning however, he had found himself standing a good foot shorter than the three men, whose expressions rendered them all capable of killing and who looked completely out of place, dwarfing the slightly uncomfortable looking, softly spoken but still attractive lady of the house who had answered the door a few moments ago and who was now trying to disappear into her seat. He didn't need to be a police inspector to know that things were tense between the three other men in the room. Taking his time he looked at each man in turn, while it seemed none of the men breathed, he then faced his colleague with his customary shrewd look and Columbo act and wished he still smoked so that he could buy some more time.

"Would you be so kind as to introduce yourselves please gentleman?" He spoke to no one in particular but kept his eyes on the two men who stood just inside the doorway feeling the room get smaller by the minute. Conrad went into automatic mode and adopting his best solicitors voice he calmly told the inspector who he was and his profession and briefly caught a look of relief from the older lady who looked visibly worried. Kian spoke next, his thick Scottish burr breaking the silence and he walked over to Anna and gently placed his hand on her shoulder to reassure her. Adam stepped forward and introduced himself as Melissa's beau and immediately the air crackled as both Conrad and Kian shot a menacing glance in Adam's direction. Anna feeling the weight of Kian's hand on her shoulder although feeling relaxed was very aware that Inspector Johnson was taking in every inch of the three men who stood in her kitchen, looking like something out of a fantasy novel and probably wondering just as she was how they had all ended up in her kitchen. Feeling the instinctive need to explain something she wasn't sure how to explain, Anna was just about to interrupt Adam before he had a chance to finish introducing himself and his reasons for being there, when Melissa came sleepy-eyed into the kitchen and the tension in the room lifted as all eyes turned towards her. Inspector Johnson's colleague was still young but even he didn't miss the change in the room as she entered and clearing his throat he looked to Inspector Johnson, momentarily lost for words as he noted the expression on the Inspectors face.

As Melissa entered the kitchen she came to an abrupt halt at the sight that greeted her. Not knowing where to look or at who to look at, she rocked backwards on her heel losing her balance and without a seconds hesitation Conrad moved swiftly to block the doorway and prevent Melissa from stepping backwards and losing her footing. As soon as her body came into contact with his all hell seemed to break loose in the kitchen. Adam and Kian both stepped forward while the inspectors young colleague jumped out of the way of the two advancing men. Inspector Johnson's hat nearly came off his head with the force of air the two men made as they moved like lightening and he only just caught the expression on Anna's face as Adam made a grab for Melissa at the same time as Kian reached for Adam to stop him. Conrad's reflexes usually so sharp deserted him as he felt Melissa lean back against him to stop herself from falling and was rendered incapable of thought or movement. In the space of a heartbeat Melissa quickly gained her footing and stepped away from Conrad into Adams arms but could still feel a fissure of heat from where she had fallen back against Conrad. Still in a daze about walking into the kitchen to find it full of people and especially two men who looked suspiciously like police officers, she looked up at Adam feeling relieved to see him and now only just truly registering the fact that Conrad Mackenzie was stood in the kitchen. She couldn't hide the look of bewilderment and surprise as she glanced at Anna looking for some sort of reassurance she wasn't dreaming.

Inspector Johnson looked at Melissa being held tightly within Adam's embrace and thought there was an unnatural air about the man, but it was Melissa's face that had caught him by surprise as he was sure that he recognised her but knew that was impossible. Still his instinct had never let him down in the years he had served in the police force and he couldn't shake the feeling that there was a lot more going on within these four walls that what met the eye. Reluctantly putting that thought away for now, he reached inside his coat and pulled out his worn leather-bound notebook, flicking over the pages as he sought a fresh page on which to write on. Tapping his pencil on the blank page to gain everyones attention he looked over at his colleague and nodded; immediately the young officer took out his own notes and the report that outlined their reason for being there. Although the tension could still be felt in the room Inspector Johnson knew he was only there to ask some routine questions and that whatever secrets these four walls held could wait. He started with Kian and worked his way around all the faces on the room gathering names and details of their whereabouts in the last few days and their reason for being in the Highlands. Despite his internal misgivings about what could be causing the atmospheric conflict he proceeded with his basic line of questioning. Satisfied that the names and addresses and reasons for being in the Highlands were genuine, he couldn't dismiss the feeling that there was a lot that wasn't being said. He didn't miss the way Mr MacKenzie bristled when Mr Donnell gave his details and nor did he mistake the looks that passed between the towering MacLeod. He looked briefly down at his note book tapping MacLeod's first name of Kian and felt the hairs on the back of his neck stand up.

He wasn't a superstitious Scot but glancing up sharply and looking between Conrad and Kian it was like looking at two Highland warriors of old. His colleagues voice seemed very distant as he went over the report of the burnt out car they had attended yesterday and what had looked like a the remains of two human bodies. But it would appear that no one here had seen any suspicious activity that they could recall and no one it appeared seemed to know of anyone who drove a Audi A6 that might have also been planning on paying a visit. He wasn't buying it... the greatest crime in the last few weeks had been old Mrs McNeill's dog going walkabout after she had left it tethered to the old post outside the local inn. Burn't cars where one thing but human remains was quite another and he hadn't missed the gleaming car that sat in the drive that he had passed on his way in to the house. He felt the urge to glance up at Kian once more and as soon as he did their eyes locked and any thoughts he had had previously, vanished and were replaced with thoughts of his wife scotch broth and warm home made bread. Speaking over his colleague who was repeating out loud the notes he was taking down. He told the room that that would be all for now and thanked them for their help. Passing his card around so that everyone had one he then turned to face Anna and like a spell that had been cast he thanked her once again and nodded at his colleague to lead the way out. As he brushed past Melissa he felt a jolt but his feet seemed to have a mind of their own and carried on taking him out of the kitchen and towards the entrance.

As he reached the entrance he stepped aside to let his young colleague pass and turned to face Kian who had silently followed them to the door and who now stood wearing the expression of not knowing if he had erred, leaving Conrad in the Kitchen with Melissa and Anna with no explanation as to how Conrad came to be there . As his palm slipped into Kian's solid grip he instantly felt the strength of ten men as Kian's hand closed around his. Kian neither squeezed nor did he exert any pressure, he just simply held Inspector Johnson's slightly damp palm within his own but through his touch he reassured the Inspector that he would not find what he was looking for here and he felt again the mans curious mind begin to question what Kian was now implanting there; just as it had when he had flipped though his notepad and had been impervious to knowing that Kian was not immune to the suspicious thoughts that had gone through the Inspectors mind. Letting go of his hand he smiled at the inspector and wished him well but felt that that would not be the last they saw of him. As the Inspector walked down the steps and towards his car he spied his young colleague who was already seated and had started the engine. He couldn't shake the feeling that he was missing something... opening the door to the passengers side he got in, still with a quizzical look on his face all he could think about was his wifes home made bread and scotch broth and instantly his stomach rumbled. Looking at his watch he noted that it was fast approaching lunchtime and thought it was no wonder his stomach had let out a growl. The morning had unusually sped by and unconsciously he patted his pocket that contained his notepad and glanced back at the house through the side mirror as his young colleague took off back down the drive. Scratching his chin Inspector Johnson still felt that something wasn't quite right but the overriding need to get home for lunch blocked out everything else. Perhaps once he had eaten it might come to him and he settled back in the seat as the car turned out of the drive and on to the deserted main road.

Kian stood and watched the Inspectors car until it had disappeared from sight and then closed the door quietly shut.

He had listened to every detail the Inspector and his colleague had spoken in the kitchen and try as he might he had no idea what or who they could be referring too. Kian had nearly lost his normal calm composure when both he and Conrad had first entered the kitchen and saw them standing there. For Kian knew exactly who they were before any introductions had been made as Kian's path had crossed the Inspectors once before, a long time ago. Not wanting to dwell on that encounter his mind had instantly switched to thoughts of Suzy and he had almost tasted blood in his mouth he had gritted his teeth so hard when they had mentioned the burnt car and its contents. It was only as Kian had probed the Inspectors mind and saw images of the bodies he relaxed as neither of them had been Suzy's but were in fact male. As the Inspectors suspicions begin to form Kian had began replacing those thoughts with different ones. However he knew from experience it was only a temporary measure as Inspector Johnson had proven to be a little unexpected. He was also very aware that Adam had remained stuck to Melissa and

Conrad's quiet rage had rolled off of him like gathering storm clouds. He needed to speak with Melissa to find out if she had seen or heard from Suzy since yesterday. For if she hadn't then Kian did not want to contemplate what that might mean. Touching the stone in his pocket he sought some kind of calm to shroud the fear that was beginning to take root.

As he stepped back in to the kitchen all eyes turned to face him and instantly he knew what was coming and as the fear began to twist its ugly self around his core he struggled to maintain an outward calm and took strength from Conrad as he felt Conrad's hand come to rest on his shoulder.

Melissa was still trying to take in the sudden unexpectedness of the Inspectors visit as it had brought back painful memories of her mothers death and as thoughts of her mother turned into thoughts of Suzy and her crazy comments which were both comical but comforting. She realised that she hadn't really given much thought to Suzy since they had arrived. She had been so wrapped up yesterday first with Anna and then with the books she had found in the library that she had just assumed that Suzy had gone off exploring, more than likely fantasying about Kian and having her wicked way. Except when Melissa had heard that awful tyre screeching horrendously loud noise and had rushed out to see what or who had caused it, she was dumbstruck when she had seen Kian standing then clean out of breath and had even joked that perhaps Suzy had already been entertaining Kian in his room and he had been embarrassed at being caught out. However she now didn't feel so sure and the realisation that she hadn't actually seen Suzy for twenty-four hours came crashing down on her like an almighty fist.

"Oh my god!" Melissa exclaimed to no one in particular and then looked expectantly at Kian and then at Adam, forgetting for a moment that Conrad was also stood in the kitchen and who had now moved over to where Anna sat and was explaining to her how he knew Melissa and that he come here with regards to her inheritance. Seeing that Anna was lost to Conrad's dark features Melissa's worried eyes searched Kian's with a wordless plea. Kian felt Melissa's eyes like shards of metal and he instinctively moved towards her with his palm facing up. Noticing Kian's sudden movement Adam pulled Melissa closer to him, stopping Kian in his tracks. Adam bent down to whisper in her ear and asked what had upset her.

"Its Suzy...I...I haven't seen her and I've only just realised how awful I have been to have been so wrapped up in the library, on you Adam and you Anna and this house that had not thought about her at all!!" She pushed away from Adam and ran past Kian who stood trying to reconstruct his innards and fought Conrad's grasp as he had risen to catch her before she could escape the room.

"She has to be upstairs...she has to be..." Melissa felt fear, real fear and couldn't explain it. How could she have not noticed her one true friend had been absent for all this time. What was wrong with her?...What the hell was Conrad doing here? Melissa thoughts questioned and crashed as she fled up the stairs and barged into the room Suzy was staying in. Close behind her was Kian followed by Conrad and Anna was struggling to keep up but had managed to remain not far behind.

Melissa sank to her knees with tears streaming down her face.

"Oh my god...where is she? Where is she Kian?....She's left and I've been so preoccupied I hadn't even noticed!" For every tear that fell down Melissa face Kian felt it leave a scar on his very soul. This was not how it was planned and he shook his head vehemently whilst bending down to raise Melissa up from her knees. Conrad stood back and felt helpless to intercept all the while he felt the stirrings of Ciar rumble within him at Melissa's clear distress. Melissa used her hands to grip Kian as she stood and steadied herself. Looking up into his face she saw her confusion mirrored there and she whispered brokenly... where is she?...

Anna prised Melissa's hands from Kian's strong forearms and held her in a motherly embrace, nodding to Kian to go and do whatever he needed to do to find out where Suzy had got too. Anna's own guilt about being as preoccupied threatened to overspill and she hugged Melissa fiercely, stroking her hair like she had once done to Melissa as a child whilst reassuring her that Kian would find Suzy, no matter what, Kian would find her, of that Anna had no doubt. In the midst of her tears, confusion and wild stare to where Suzy's few belongings lay haphazardly around the room Melissa looked over Anna shoulder expecting to see Adam. All she saw was Conrad's wild eyes staring back at her. Forcing her mouth to work while he was fixated on her was not easy but she croaked out Adam's name and saw Conrad's expression turn from wild to thunderous and she unconsciously shrank back from the two pools of explosive, molten silver that were beginning to engulf her. Screwing her eyes shut and with a confidence she didn't feel, she then forced them open to stare back at Conrad with the same fierce determination she felt coming from his and caught the back of him as he left the doorway to Suzy's room. She slumped in Anna's arms praying in between sobs that Suzy would turn up and laugh at them all. Or that god forbid Kian would find her wherever she had got to and that she would be safe. This was all her fault. As she squeezed her eyes shut one more time she pictured the two charred bodies the police had mentioned in an abandoned car and her mothers face appeared followed by Suzy's. Oh god...please no...this can not be...it simply can not be... Melissa abruptly broke free of Anna's embrace and ran out of the room to find Adam.

CHAPTER TWENTY-NINE

As she appeared in the human realm she realised her error. For as she took on the form of the cat she immediately sensed that he was here. How was that possible?...She had never felt his presence before when she had entered this realm. Flicking her tail she ran across the grass and snuck behind the hedgerow. His aura of dark menace was everywhere. Her tail swished side to side and up against the hedge row in agitation and instead of raising a paw to her mouth to gracefully lick it in self satisfaction she arched her back and dug her claws into the soft earth. This could not happen... She could not let this happen... She bore witness to her predecessors, who were now trapped entities, every one hundred years and although some looked upon her in awe for outwitting the dark master for longer than all the rest. Others would look at her with the sure knowledge of what fate finally awaited her. She could not let that happen... She would not let that happen... and with that she ran on all fours back towards the house and jumped up on to one of the large sills and peered through the glass. In the room she spied Anna, whom she had visited several times before, looking nervous and surrounded by several people. Purring she noted the watcher and her soul were reunited. This meant she was close...so close... Slanting her sleek neck to one side she then padded along the sill so that she could see better who else was also stood in the room. As she glanced back through the glass she misted the glass as her nose pressed up against its cold surface and then she saw the dark aura. Fear struck at her very core...No...No...No... not now...NO... fighting the urge to transform she watched helplessly as the men ran from the room chasing the woman and the dark aura was gone.

His vapour swirled restlessly around the base of the cherry tree and he watched her leap up on to the sill. Graceful as ever even in animal form he angrily admired her form as she leapt. He was so close...so close...he could not lose...he would not lose this time. His existence was infinite and in over a millennia he never questioned, never believed, never felt...never won... he just was. Was that why he had now started to question...started to believe...was it because he was so close...had it changed things?...He knew she felt him for he felt her. He wondered briefly if she would look to where he had invaded each blossom as his essence had brushed past it, turning their petals from pink to charred black. Then as he sifted through the air to materialise as close to her as he dared he thought better of it and in his internal struggle he hung back unsure why and remained like cloud of dust, hovering just above the damp earth.

She sprang from the sill and she landed with a gentle thud. She was drawn to the cherry tree and in the space that separated them she willed herself not to use magic for it would be like a beacon to a lost ship. She knew he felt her as she did feel him. Her cats eyes narrowed to slits as she peered across the earth that stood between them and saw the glistening of the ground just in front of the tree. The only sound was her heart beat as it pounded evenly within her chest. Resisting the urge to change form she stood, unmoving until the dust rematerialised and a man stood under the tree, his piercing gaze daring and full of triumph stared right back at her.

As one they both turned in the direction of the house at the sound of tyres on the gravel over and above raised voices. Time was suspended as she broke all the rules and transformed into her natural glamour and as she did so she dared a look in his direction, the pull of his power equal to her own was like a magnetic mirror. With an immediate sweep of his hand he too changed into his natural glamour so that both of them were undetectable in this realm but were vulnerable to each others essence. She would lose this time... Playing her at her own game would be her undoing.

Adam had remained calm and had answered the police officers questions but as soon as Melissa had cried Suzy's name he knew he had to act quickly. Luckily for him that hulk of a Scot left with the drip of a solicitor chasing his tail so he managed to slip unnoticed out of the kitchen and out the front entrance while the rest ran up to the first floor and Anna had remained seated in the kitchen, muttering to herself. As he got into his car he drove off kicking up gravel as he made his exit and to where he had thought he had left Suzy. Driven by an incessant need to reach Suzy but unfamiliar with the roads he nearly lost the car on the sharp hazardous bends that mapped the distance he travelled away from the house. Slowing down he tried to remember any give away landmarks that would tell him he was close but everything looked the same. Adam was blind to the mountains that stood either side of him covered in glorious wild purple heather and that had rivulets of water which, cascaded down various contours of each majestic rock. All he saw were mountains that threatened to swallow him up and that were grey, bleak and covered in a dark heavy mist. The oppressive darkness that did indeed engulf the car and its occupant , drifted slightly allowing a glimpse of a track that veered off of the road and without hesitation Adam swung the car of the road and followed the track feeling at last he knew where he was headed and with a sneer he could almost taste victory. All he had to do was finish Suzy once and for all and go back to Melissa to help and comfort her over the loss of her friend, although a very small part of him fought the compulsion of evil that he knew he was capable of he had learned from a very young age, it was at the centre of his very core and could do nothing but embrace the rushing feeling of power that consumed him.

Kian needed no prompting from Anna as he dimly felt her fingers prising Melissa off of him. Rage threatened to manifest itself in all of its ugly facets and reveal a side of him he did not wish folk to be a party too. Instead he strode from

Suzy's bedroom and took the stairs two at a time, heading straight for the Kitchen. It was about time he questioned Adam. As he rounded the corner to the kitchen with the question already leaving his lips, he stopped short as Adam was nowhere to be seen. Battling to keep the vicious rage from finally getting out he used every ounce of magic he dared to calm his inner beast and opened his mind outwards. Adams essence had left the barest of trails and at first Kian had difficultly pinpointing in which direction Adam had left the house. Following the faint trail he walked back the way he had came and towards the main entrance. As he was about to open the door he felt Conrad's hand grab his arm to pull him back.

"You need to explain a lot more than what you have told me... Who is Suzy and why has she set you so on edge?" Conrad words broke through Kian's trance like state and not having the time or inclination to explain what he couldn't even begin explaining to himself he looked down at where Conrad's strong grip held him and spoke in almost a whisper.

"Come with me."

Conrad relaxed his grip and nodded his assent and followed Kian out of the house and around the side towards where Kian kept his Harley. Conrad couldn't help but let out a grin and swiftly bought the spare helmet Kian tossed at him.

"Donna be talking tae mi... Just follow wha' I tell ye." Kian didn't make a request he simply made a statement and Conrad nodded once and swung his leg over the bike while fastening his helmet strap under his chin. Only just gripping the back bar on the seat as Kian kicked the bike into a roar and then used his power to pick up the faint trail left by Adam's essence. A thought kept niggling at Kian regarding Adams faint essence but so focused on following the tiny threads, that floated unseen to the human eye to find where he had fled too, that he didn't look back over his shoulder and see magical sparks rising up in the air and coming from underneath the blossom tree.

Adam pulled up in front of the old disused bothy and let himself in flashing the torch on his phone on and pointing into the corner where he had left Suzy tied up. Sensing the light but feeling weak and tired it hurt Suzy to look up. Adam looked down at Suzy and couldn't believe how easy this was going to be. First Winchester now Suzy, finally Melissa would be his and there was no one else to stop him. Fleetingly he thought of Conrad, that solicitor who had so rudely shown up where he was least wanted and at such a crucial time in his plan. Never mind he thought, as soon as he was finished here he would go back to the house and get rid of Conrad. Suzy cracked open her eye and couldn't quite make out who it was until he spoke her name.

Her insides screamed for release but fear kept her mouth shut as she watched through half opened eyes Adam pace around the small space surrounding them both. She had no idea how long she had been here or indeed what the time was. The smell of urine reached her nose and a tear rolled sown her check as she realised that it was her own urine she could smell. She breathed slowly and silently so as not to break his pacing while she tried to think of how she could escape.

Kian drove like the ghost rider, the threads becoming thicker and longer the nearer he got to Adam's location. Pulling off the road and onto a dirt track he sensed magic all around him but kept his foot down, driven by the need to get to Adam. Conrad felt the shift in Kian as soon as they turned off the road and on to the dirt track. Conrad was sure he could hear whispering voices coming from behind him but when he looked over his shoulder he saw no one and shook his head not really expecting to but sure of what he could hear he tapped Kian's shoulder forcing him to slow down. As Kian slowed he too began to hear whispers and reluctantly slowed down even more and finally came to a stop close to where the bothy lay hidden amongst the magical mist. . He had heard that voice only a few times in his entire existence and now that he closed his eyes and looked about him using his mind he saw her sparkle, bright flashes of iridescent hues glistening just ahead. As sure as he was it was truly his maker he still gave pause while trying to assimilate her reasons for being here. As far as he knew she was not supposed to show herself. Cutting the engine to the bike he kicked back so that the stand flicked out and brought the bike to an abrupt stop and also enabled him to dismount. For some reason Conrad stayed silent and Kian was glad as he didn't feel up to explaining anymore this night. Looking through the mist he saw the outline of a bothy and instantly his senses became more alert as he could feel a dark presence sifting through the mist and taking form opposite his maker.

Although Conrad was silent he knew he had heard a whisper and with his newly acquired knowledge he too sensed that there was magic surrounding them both. Feeling like it was the most natural thing in the world he took a step forward and watching Kian's back, his shoulders rise and fall with each slow, steady breath Conrad began to open his senses to test what his instinct was telling him he could do.

Kian felt Conrad open up and without turning back silently made his way towards the bothy, Conrad keeping pace silently behind him.

She had broken all the rules and knew that he sensed her. Knowing she had risked all did not comfort her but instead it filled her with fear of what was yet to come. All she could do now was put her faith in the watcher and pray that she would win this battle. Sending what she dared she gave her soul a small gift and prayed that she had done enough. As he materialised the same time as her just beyond the bothy he knew that the game was near its end. Instead of the taste of final victory he felt the human emotion of disillusionment and let out a silent curse. Although bored of his existence and continual failure he had began to question, something he had never done in his entire existence. This changed the game play he thought as for the first time in over a millennia he...felt something... something that he never thought conceivable let alone even possible. He knew that she was here. He also knew that the watchers and one of the souls were here, so how should he play it? Should he play to win or should he lose once more, so that he could examine what was happening to him in more depth? The decision was taken from him as he saw a flash of her glamour just before she disappeared. He shifted form several times in frustration and anger that because of this weakness he hadn't acted and won the game easily, but instead had manipulated things beyond care and now the consequences would play out with out her bearing witness to its conclusion.

Kian forced the door to the bothy open and not needing a torchlight to see inside of this cruel, cold damp, dark place he sensed Suzy in the far corner and the presence of Adam directly in from of him. Both at once Adam and Kian clashed in the centre of the tiny space. Fists and feet lashed out in a what only could be described as a show of raw physical power. Conrad had ducked in to the bothy behind Kian and as soon as Kian had launched himself at Adam he'd gone straight over to where he dimly saw a hunched body on the floor over in the corner. When he reached Suzy she began to sob her thanks and kept apologising over and over again for the state she was in, so mortified that she had lost her dignity. Without giving it a thought Conrad reached around Suzy's back and frantically pulled and tugged at the rope that bound her to the floor. In Suzy's struggles the rope had loosened only a fraction but not enough for her to slip her hands through. Conrad aware that both Kian and Adam where practically knocking down walls in their bid to overpower one another, worked as quickly as he could to free Suzy and get her out of there. Using strength that seemed to flow down his arms and into his hands he snapped the rope in two, freeing Suzy with a fearfully ecstatic sigh and picking her up in a half run manhandled her towards the door of the bothy, whilst trying to avoid Kian and Adam who were still in hand to hand combat.

Once outside he heard Kian's voice in his head just telling him to go , get out of there and take Suzy with him. Momentarily torn between taking Suzy as far away as he could and to safety and feeling Ciar stirring within, vying for battle he itched to get back to help Kian finish Adam. Kian roared in his head which sent Conrad into automatic pilot and knowing that Kian was more than capable he placed Suzy's arms around his middle and sped off back down the track.

Their breaths came heavy and fast and Kian and Adam circled one another in the tight, cold, dark, damp space. Kian instantly felt the sudden loss of magic and having no time to wonder that could mean he just managed to duck a punch that Adam threw. Adam suddenly felt all his strength ebb and in trying to control his own breathing stumbled backwards. Kian appeared right in front of Adam and taking the dirk from its hidden location inside his shirt, in one swift motion placed it against Adam's neck. The only sound was of their breathing and of Adam's heartbeat as it pounded rapidly within his chest. Kian, paused just for a second, as he looked into the eyes of the man who had sort to hurt his twin and who had sort to gain Melissa's hand by sheer malice and deceit. In that moment while his mind was open and probing Adams own he saw for the first time genuine fear and in a slow steady motion slid the dirk across Adam's neck also realising at that very moment that the dark aura that had surrounded Adam had also gone.

As Adam slipped to the ground his eyes held Kian's with confusion until Kian turned away from him, The sound of Adam choking on his own blood rang in his ears as he walked away. Once outside of the bothy Kian stood listening with all of his senses for Adams final breath and as soon as he heard it he closed his eyes and looked heavenward. It was then he realised that this place would never be seen by human eyes. For he could feel the magic vibrating beneath his feet and having no option but to get into Adams car and go back to Caberfeidh he watched in the rearview mirror the bothy disappear from sight, taking with it any evidence of Adams existence.

CHAPTER THIRTY

Printed in Great Britain
by Amazon.co.uk, Ltd.,
Marston Gate.